Tenerife
& La Gomera

DIRECTIONS

WRITTEN AND RESEARCHED BY

Christian Williams

ROUGH
GUIDES

NEW YORK • LONDON • DELHI
www.roughguides.com

Contents

Introduction to

Tenerife
& La Gomera

Despite glorious weather and a variety of landscapes that attract four million tourists every year, Tenerife has an image problem. Thanks to package tourism, the entire island is assumed to be a playground for rowdy holiday-makers, content to spend lazy days on the beach and drink-fuelled nights in the bars and if this is what you're after, you won't be disappointed. But get off the beaten track and you'll discover spectacular volcanic scenery, elegant resorts and peaceful Spanish towns. And with the island measuring just 86km long and 56km wide, everywhere is a possible day-trip.

▲ La Orotava

Some of the most memorable sights are natural ones – the most impressive being around the island's pre-eminent landmark, the volcano Mount Teide. The turbulent history of the islands has left a host of sights that deserve a look too. Traces of the original inhabitants, the **Guanche**, can be found at various sites around the islands, while the impact of the Spanish conquest is best seen in their colonial towns which offer a complete contrast to the brash, more recently developed resorts.

◄ Playa de Las Américas

Though Tenerife has many peaceful areas, those wanting to get even further away from the crowds should head to the strikingly precipitous island of La Gomera. A 28km ferry-ride from Tenerife, it was the first of the Canary Islands to be conquered by the Spanish (Tenerife was the last) and is also the greenest and least populated of the archipelago, bisected by deep ravines that radiate out from its centre. The absence of major beaches – and, consequently, resorts – means laid-back rural tranquillity is still intact here, making it a relaxing place for a break.

▲ San Francisco Convent, Garachico

When to visit

The climate across the Canary Islands is mild year-round, with relatively minimal seasonal change. That said, southern areas of both Tenerife and La Gomera see most sun and record the higher temperatures, while the north tends to be cooler, with more rainfall. Inland from the coast, higher terrain means temperatures become progressively colder, with Tenerife's Mount Teide often experiencing freezing temperatures and occasional snow cover. High season is during the European winter, and places get especially busy from mid-December to February, when temperatures hover around 20°C. The islands are also popular at Easter and during summer holidays (June–Sept) when temperatures can get up to 30°C. A low season of sorts exists between these times, with the notable exception of the carnival period (Feb or March), when Santa Cruz is at its busiest.

›› TENERIFE & LA GOMERA AT A GLANCE

Santa Cruz and La Laguna

The best places to immerse yourself in Canarian culture, Tenerife's present and former capitals offer the chance to experience traditional architecture, local cuisine, lively nightlife and one of the world's biggest carnivals.

Courtyard interior, Santa Cruz

Lago Martianez, Puerto de la Cruz

Playa de Las Américas, Los Cristianos and the Costa Adeje

A gigantic resort on the sunniest part of the island, with strings of hotels, restaurants and bars, many lining the island's major artificial beaches. Vulgar, hedonistic and – if this is your kind of thing – great fun.

Los Cristianos

Puerto de la Cruz and La Orotava

Puerto, the island's oldest resort, first became fashionable over a century ago and today offers a more genteel alternative to the southern resorts. Close by, in the island's most fertile valley, La Orotava's former wealth as an agricultural centre is evidenced by its grand houses.

Mount Teide and the interior

The 3718-metre high volcano Mount Teide is the highest point on Spanish territory and symbol of Tenerife. Standing in a national park at the centre of a vast tree-less volcanic wasteland of twisted lava, it's encircled by damp and often misty Canarian pine forest.

Northern La Gomera

Cool and damp northern La Gomera is better suited to banana plantations than tourist resorts, with slow-paced rural villages remaining relatively untouched. The area's highlight though is the Parque Nacional de Garajonay, a UNESCO World Heritage Site containing the world's premium laurel forest.

◀ Flora, Mount Teide National Park

◀ View from Garajonay

Ideas

The big six sights

As well as a generally warm and sunny climate, Tenerife's and La Gomera's attractions also include a "big six sights" that any visitor should try to see. From spectacular **natural wonders** providing physical reminders of a turbulent geological past, to the **architectural legacy** of the original Guanche inhabitants and the Spanish colonizers, the islands offer enough interest to get even the most devout sun worshipper off the beach.

Dragon Tree, Icod de Los Viños

Guanche elders once held meetings under this proud old tree – the largest of its kind – but now it's visitors who flock here.

▶ P.92 ▶ GARACHICO ▲

Carnival

Europe's biggest and liveliest carnival celebrations begin in Santa Cruz before continuing across Tenerife.

▶ P.172 ▶ ESSENTIALS ▲

Teide

Dominating Tenerife and visible from virtually every point on the island, volcanic Mount Teide has an overpowering allure.

▸ P.135 ▸ MOUNT TEIDE AND THE INTERIOR ▲

Doce Casas

View the beautiful mansions of the merchants who grew rich trading the bountiful harvests of La Orotava valley in the seventeenth and eighteenth centuries.

▸ P.85 ▸ LA OROTAVA ▼

Laurel Forest, Garajonay

Enter an ancient, overgrown ecosystem where laurels and mosses thrive.

▸ P.157 ▸ NORTHERN LA GOMERA ▲

Los Roques de García

A mesmerizing outcrop of warped rock, rising up from an otherwise flat plain in the shadow of Mount Teide.

▸ P.133 ▸ MOUNT TEIDE AND THE INTERIOR ▼

Tenerife in a week

A week on Tenerife gives you enough time to sample the island's variety. A stay wouldn't be complete without a day on a **beach** and an evening spent eating freshly caught **fish**, while day-trips provide the chance to see **whales** and dolphins or ancient **pyramids**. The most spectacular excursion is to **Mount Teide** and its national park, with magnificent views over the Canarian archipelago and the chance to do some hiking.

Pirámides de Güímar

The pyramids present an enigmatic snapshot of ancient history and are the most significant relic of the indigenous Guanche society.

▸ P.72 ▸ CANDELARIA AND GÜÍMAR   ▲

Tan on a beach

Unwind, soak up some rays, read a book and go for a paddle.

▸ P.107 ▸ LOS CRISTIANOS, LAS AMÉRICAS AND COSTA ADEJE   ▲

Hike in the Canarian pine forest

Take in the fresh air and marvel at the unique Canarian pine trees in this atmospheric forest.

▸ P.129 ▸ MOUNT TEIDE AND
THE INTERIOR ▼

Eat seafood in Los Abrigos

Pick whichever freshly caught fish takes your fancy in the restaurants of Los Abrigos, a village famous for its excellent seafood.

▸ P.128 ▸ THE SOUTH COAST ▼

Visit Parque Nacional del Teide

Dramatic lunar landscapes and Spain's highest peak make a visit to this national park a must.

▸ P.129 ▸ MOUNT TEIDE AND
THE INTERIOR ▲

After midnight

It's after midnight that Tenerife's **nightlife** really starts. Avoid the seedy clubs aimed squarely at the tourist market in Las Américas and head instead to the bars frequented by locals, where the atmosphere is more cheerful and relaxed. The student scene in La Laguna is particularly welcoming.

Malibu Beach

The best in a strip of busy late-night clubs along Santa Cruz's Avenida Anaga.

▶ P.59 ▶ SANTA CRUZ ▲

Bobby's, Las Américas

Busy club, at the centre of the action on the Las Veronicas strip.

▶ P.120 ▶ LOS CRISTIANOS, LAS AMÉRICAS AND COSTA ADEJE ▲

Metropolis

Big two-storey club, with several
dance floors and a cosmopolitan
clientele.

▶ P.120 ▶ LOS CRISTIANOS, LAS
AMÉRICAS AND COSTA ADEJE ▲

Tropicana

Cuban dance show followed by Latin-
style partying into the early hours.

▶ P.120 ▶ LOS CRISTIANOS, LAS
AMÉRICAS AND COSTA ADEJE ▶

El Buho

One of La Laguna's premier venues
for live music.

▶ P.65 ▶ LA LAGUNA ▼

Shopping and souvenirs

Low sales tax makes Tenerife and La Gomera something of a **shopper's paradise** with hundreds of small outlets in the resorts selling everything from jewellery and perfume to electrical gadgetry. More traditional souvenirs include wooden carvings, basketware, pottery, embroidery and lacework, cigars and novelty liqueurs. Also worth looking out for is honey taken from hives around Teide, the islands' goats cheeses and *mojo*, the favourite local dip. Opening hours in the resorts and larger towns are typically daily 8am to 8pm; the rest of the islands keep more restricted hours (usually Mon–Sat 9am–1pm & 4–8pm).

Flea Market, Santa Cruz

For unusual souvenirs, head for the flea-market held outside Santa Cruz's Mercado de Nuestra Señora de África on Sunday mornings.

▶ P.57 ▶ SANTA CRUZ

Lace

Two traditions of fine lace-making are practised in Tenerife – techniques in La Orotava use a wooden frame while elsewhere small rosettes are sewn together to form larger pieces.

▶ P.87 ▶ LA OROTAVA

Mercado de Nuestra Señora de África

Santa Cruz's bustling, Moorish-style covered market sells mostly groceries and is a great place to pick up inexpensive local produce, particularly cheeses.

▶ P.57 ▶ SANTA CRUZ ▶

Cigars

Offering Cuban quality at less expensive prices, it's easy to see why Tenerife's cigars were Winston Churchill's favourites.

▶ P.57 ▶ SANTA CRUZ ▼

Los Cristianos

The pedestrian core of Los Cristianos has an array of luxury goods outlets from electrical appliances to perfume shops.

▶ P.110 ▶ LOS CRISTIANOS, LAS AMÉRICAS AND COSTA ADEJE ▼

Pots, Las Hayas

Traditional hardwearing pots, produced by hand from a single lump of clay as they have been for centuries.

▶ P.163 ▶ NORTHERN LA GOMERA ▼

Cafés and bars

In common with mainland Spain, Tenerife and La Gomera have a lively café and bar culture. Food and alcohol are served in both, blurring distinctions between the two, though generally **cafés** specialize in cakes and sandwiches, while **bars** – also called *tascas*, *bodegas*, *cervecerías* and *tabernas* – have a greater range of alcoholic drinks and tapas. Bars called *areperas* serve South American *arepas* – deep-fried pockets of cornmeal dough stuffed with chicken, cheese or ham. Most cafés and bars open long hours, typically 8am–midnight, so in the text we give hours only when they differ greatly from this.

Cacatua

An institution in Valle Gran Rey, this airy bar has a tropical feel and great cocktails.

▶ P.156 ▶ VALLE GRAN REY ▲

El Pingüino

Arguably the best ice-cream on the island in a large variety of flavours.

▶ P.83 ▶ PUERTO DE LA CRUZ ▲

La Casa Vieja

Basic tapas in a no-frills bar on one of the backstreets of La Gomera's capital.

▶ P.147 ▶ SAN SEBASTIÁN ▼

Harley's American Diner

Americana in Las Américas, with the chance to sip drinks in a Cadillac.

▶ P.119 ▶ LOS CRISTIANOS, LAS AMÉRICAS AND COSTA ADEJE ▲

Playa Chica

Great little locals' tapas bar, with a tiny patio looking out to sea.

▶ P.128 ▶ THE SOUTH COAST ▲

Flashpoint

Favoured by windsurfers, this place has a patio overlooking the beach and a laid-back atmosphere.

▶ P.127 ▶ THE SOUTH COAST ▶

Romantic Tenerife

An island best known for package tours might seem an odd choice for a romantic break. But Tenerife does contain some hidden-away, rural retreats, far off the beaten track, where couples can enjoy the peace and quiet. And with sun, sea and warm temperatures, there are plenty of opportunities for sunset strolls and candlelit dinners by the ocean.

Casas Rurales

These "rural houses" in isolated locations are the perfect hideaway for couples seeking solitude amid natural beauty.

▶ P.174 ▶ ESSENTIALS ▲

Promenade, Las Américas

Forget the hotel complexes behind you and enjoy the seaward views from Las Américas' promenade.

▶ P.111 ▶ LOS CRISTIANOS, LAS AMÉRICAS AND COSTA ADEJE ▲

Parador Nacionál de Cañadas del Teide

Treat yourself and your beloved to a splurge in this luxury hotel, with its stunning backdrop of the national park and Mount Teide.

▶ P.137 ▶ MOUNT TEIDE AND THE INTERIOR ▲

La Caleta

This small, peaceful fishing village is a great spot for some al fresco dining while the sun sets over the ocean.

▶ P.112 ▶ LOS CRISTIANOS, LAS AMÉRICAS AND COSTA ADEJE ▼

Tambara

Good food, good views and hopefully good vibrations at this small La Gomeran café-bar.

▶ P.155 ▶ VALLE GRAN REY ▶

Luxury Tenerife

There are plenty of chances to splurge and pamper yourself in Tenerife. Many options are to be found in the **five-star hotels** and their **restaurants**, but there are also some unique ways to sightsee during your trip, from cruising on a **yacht** to getting a bird's-eye view from a **plane**.

Charter a yacht

Let others do the work while you laze on deck, take a dip or look out for dolphins.

▶ P.171 ▶ ESSENTIALS ▲

Hotel Mencey

Stylish, elegant accommodation in Tenerife's capital with everything you'd expect from one of the island's best hotels.

▶ P.55 ▶ SANTA CRUZ ▲

Flightseeing

If money is no object, then a flight over Tenerife provides unforgettable views of the island – don't forget your camera.

▸ P.170 ▸ ESSENTIALS ▲

Restaurante Piramide

Lively opera nights, superb food and unobtrusive service make this a great place for a splurge.

▸ P.119 ▸ LOS CRISTIANOS, LAS AMÉRICAS AND COSTA ADEJE ◂

Suite at the Sir Anthony

Spacious suites, sea views and private gardens, plus the attentive service of a small hotel.

▸ P.116 ▸ LOS CRISTIANOS, LAS AMÉRICAS AND COSTA ADEJE ▸

A spa treatment at the Mare Nostrum

Indulge yourself with a range of beauty treatments. A day of pampering costs €85, including use of pool, saunas and gym.

▸ P.116 ▸ LOS CRISTIANOS, LAS AMÉRICAS AND COSTA ADEJE ▼

Restaurants

Most traditional Canarian restaurants serve simple meals at moderate prices – €6–8 per main dish – and are broadly divided into those by the coast offering mainly **fish** and **seafood**, and inland establishments that tend to specialize in **meat** dishes. **Opening hours** are generally 1–4pm & 8pm–midnight, though in the resorts, places serving largely pan-European food open from 10am to 10pm. In reviews we've listed opening hours only for establishments with unusual hours.

L'Alpage

Off the beaten track Swiss restaurant that faithfully reproduces alpine cooking.

▸ P.127 ▸ THE SOUTH COAST

Pizzería Rugantino

Simple restaurant, fabulous pizzas.

▸ P.95 ▸ GARACHICO

Maquila

Tasty Canarian food at reasonable prices, off the tourist trail.

▶ P.64 ▶ LA LAGUNA ▲

Natural Burguer

Popular with students, this burger bar has a wide range of tasty options at budget prices.

▶ P.64 ▶ LA LAGUNA ▼

La Rosa di Bari

Highly recommended place with wonderful food, elegant surroundings and efficient service.

▶ P.84 ▶ PUERTO DE LA CRUZ ▼

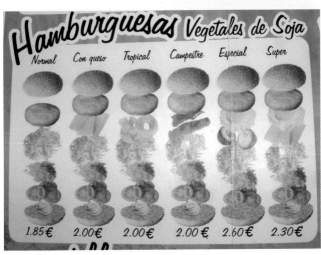

Food and drink

Fresh fish and seafood provide one of the culinary highlights of a visit to Tenerife and La Gomera. Paellas using the local catch are common on the islands, as is the traditional Canarian fish stew, *zarzuela*. Specialities of the interior include the rich *conejo en salmorejo* – marinated rabbit in a garlicky sauce. Both fish and meat are generally grilled and served with **papas arrugadas**, a typically Canarian potato dish. Occasionally vegetables or a pitiful side salad are served along with the potatoes, and the presence of **mojo** can be virtually guaranteed. To wash it all down, there's a good range of Canarian **wines** and **beers** and a great local rum.

Ron Miel

A honey rum drink, made on the islands and ideal for those with a sweet tooth. Served in bars and restaurants everywhere, it's best enjoyed watching the sunset.

▶ P.128 ▶ PLAYA CHICA, THE SOUTH COAST ▲

Dorada

Refreshing and ubiquitous Tenerife lager, downed by the gallon in Las Américas.

▶ P.119 ▶ LOS CRISTIANOS, LAS AMÉRICAS AND COSTA ADEJE ▲

Mojo

This garlic dip comes in two varieties: spicy *rojo* (red), made with chillies; or milder *verde* (green), made with coriander. To many Canarians the quality of its *mojo* is the measure of a restaurant.

▶ P.147 ▶ CUBINO, SAN SEBASTIÁN ◀

Wines

Tenerife has a decent range of dry white wines. Look out for *Viña Norte*, characterized by its fruity flavour, and wines from El Sauzal such as the *Viñatigo*, known for their crisp freshness.

▶ P.80 ▶ PUERTO DE LA CRUZ ▶

Papas arrugadas

A speciality of the Canary Islands, these unpeeled new potatoes, boiled dry in salt water, are a delicious accompaniment to fresh seafood.

▶ P.147 ▶ SAN SEBASTIÁN ▼

Gofio

A finely ground mixture of roasted wheat, maize or barley, this Canarian staple is regularly offered in place of bread.

▶ P.164 ▶ SONIA, NORTHERN LA GOMERA ▲

Culture

Developing in the shadow of mainland Spain and as a vital transatlantic crossroads, the Canaries eclectic influences have helped to create a unique culture. To experience what the islands have to offer there are several **venues** putting on performances, or for a taste of traditional life, seek out one of the many **festivals**.

Pot making, Las Hayas, La Gomera

Pre-Hispanic crafts are still produced in La Gomera's uplands.

▸ P.163 ▸ NORTHERN LA GOMERA ▲

Marqués de Cristano

For the chance to try authentic Canarian food, this La Gomeran restaurant, housed in an eighteenth-century house, is the place to come.

▸ P.147 ▸ SAN SEBASTIÁN ▲

Canarian dancing

Folk dancing in traditional costume can best be seen during the many festivals on the islands.

▶ **P.172** ▶
ESSENTIALS ▶

Teatro Guimerá

Traditional arts venue with a good, mixed programme.

▶ **P.60** ▶
SANTA CRUZ ◀

Canarian wrestling

Team wrestling, Canarian style, and found only on the islands.

▶ **P.172** ▶
SANTA CRUZ ▼

Museums

Tenerife's museums concentrate on the island's culture and history and are worth seeking out if you're nearby. One museum that shouldn't be missed is Santa Cruz's Museo de la Naturaleza y el Hombre, one of the government-run museums that offer a reduction in admission if you have a bono bus card (see p.168).

Museo de la Naturaleza y el Hombre

The place to head for an overview of Tenerife's nature. The Guanches are well covered and there's the chance to view some of their mummified remains.

▶ P.54 ▶ SANTA CRUZ

Museo de Bellas Artes

Tenerife's main art gallery has a small permanent collection of coins and sculptures and also attracts an interesting range of temporary exhibitions.

▶ P.51 ▶ SANTA CRUZ

Museo de la Historia de Tenerife

The place to head for an overview of Tenerife's history, with well presented displays on the Guanches particularly worth a look.

▶ P.62 ▶
LA LAGUNA ▶

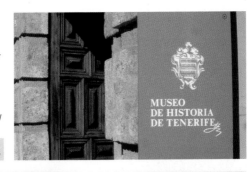

Casa Del Vino La Baranda, El Sauzal

Informative exhibition on Tenerife's long-standing wine industry, with the chance for a bit of sampling too.

▶ P.80 ▶ PUERTO DE LA CRUZ ▼

Museo Militar

Hundreds of military exhibits, enlivened by interesting insights into Nelson's failed attack on Santa Cruz.

▶ P.54 ▶ SANTA CRUZ ▲

Churches

The churches of Tenerife and La Gomera are generally simple affairs. Their most distinctive touch is the blending of eastern and western styles, with traditional church architecture complemented by Islamic-influenced *Mudéjar* ceilings. Churches with no fixed opening times generally open an hour before mass when you're welcome to have a look inside if you're discreet.

Iglesia de la Concepción

Tenerife's oldest church has a fine coffered ceiling and historic baptism font.

▶ P.63 ▶ LA LAGUNA ▲

Basilica de Nuestra Señora de Candelaria

Grand church housing a statue of the Virgin Mary that was once a Guanche idol and is now the holiest relic in the Canaries.

▶ P.71 ▶ CANDELARIA AND GÜÍMAR ▲

Santa Iglesia Cathedral

Imposing Baroque and Gothic cathedral, situated in Tenerife's original capital.

▸ P.62 ▸
LA LAGUNA ▲

Iglesia de Nuestra Señora de la Concepcion

Santa Cruz's main church displays pieces of the cross planted by Tenerife's Spanish conquerors.

▸ P.51 ▸
SANTA CRUZ ◂

Iglesia de la Virgin de la Candelaria, Chipude

Simple church with many Moorish touches, in the shadow of Mount Fortaleza.

▸ P.162 ▸ NORTHERN
LA GOMERA ▸

Landmarks

Tenerife boasts several impressive and unique natural landmarks, including Spain's highest peak, **Teide**, easily accessed by cable car or, for the energetic, on foot. The towns too have their own eye-catching architectural gems, including some striking examples of **modern architecture**.

Parque Eólico, El Medano

A windfarm-cum-visitor centre that dominates this area and offers an insight into renewable energy.

▸ P.125 ▸ THE SOUTH COAST ▲

El Drago

This ancient tree in Icod is one of Tenerife's main symbols.

▸ P.93 ▸ GARACHICO ▲

Casino Taoro

Built in 1889, this was Puerto de la Cruz's first hotel catering for tourists. The building is now a casino and stands in a commanding position above the town.

▶ P.78 ▶ PUERTO DE LA CRUZ ▲

Teide

Visible on a clear day from across the Canarian archipelago, this active volcano is Tenerife's ultimate symbol.

▶ P.135 ▶ MOUNT TEIDE AND THE INTERIOR ▶

Auditorio

Santa Cruz's most elegant landmark has equally impressive acoustics, making it a great venue for all kinds of performances.

▶ P.54 ▶ SANTA CRUZ ◀

Mare Nostrum

This huge holiday complex's extravagant architecture makes it Las Américas' most eye-catching sight.

▶ P.116 ▶ LOS CRISTIANOS, LAS AMÉRICAS AND COSTA ADEJE ▼

Outdoor activities

For sporty types, the Canary Islands have a wide range of options for an action-packed holiday. From **hiking** and **golf** to **cycling** and **volleyball**, both Tenerife and La Gomera offer an abundance of outdoor activities, most of which are possible year-round thanks to consistently fine weather.

Golf

Tenerife is ideal for a winter golf fix with more than half a dozen established and well-maintained courses.

▶ P.171 ▶ ESSENTIALS ▲

Cycling

With roads and tracks crisscrossing Tenerife, there's plenty of scope for exploring the island by bike. The steep climbs on La Gomera make them the preserve of the very fit.

▶ P.169 ▶ ESSENTIALS ▲

Fishing

You don't need a permit to join the locals in one of their favourite pastimes.

▶ P.171 ▶ ESSENTIALS ▼

Volleyball

Volleyball nets can be found on several beaches in Tenerife – particularly in Los Cristianos – and provide the chance to try out your skills.

▶ P.110 ▶ LOS CRISTIANOS, LAS AMÉRICAS AND COSTA ADEJE ▼

Hiking

When you want to get away from the crowds, it's easy to find hiking trails through spectacular scenery on both islands.

▶ P.171 ▶ ESSENTIALS ▲

Kids' Tenerife

A family holiday destination for over fifty years, Tenerife has risen to the challenge of catering for kids. All the **resorts** are child-friendly and many **commercial ventures** offer entertainment. Aside from the manmade attractions, there are also many natural ones – rock pools, beaches, mountains and forests – which can be just as much fun.

Parque las Aguilas

Top southern Tenerife attraction where if the kids get bored of the zoo and its lush vegetation, they can tire themselves out on the assault course

▶ P.114 ▶ LOS CRISTIANOS, LAS AMÉRICAS AND COSTA ADEJE ▲

Aquapark Octopus

Big, lively water park with slides and dolphin shows.

▶ P.111 ▶ LOS CRISTIANOS, LAS AMÉRICAS AND COSTA ADEJE ▲

Parques Exóticas

Children love being able to get into the enclosures with the birds and animals at this zoo.

▸ P.114 ▸ LOS CRISTIANOS, LAS AMÉRICAS AND COSTA ADEJE ▲

Karting

Budding junior Schumachers can test their road skills at this Karting centre.

▸ P.175 ▸ ESSENTIALS ▼

Loro Parque

The parrots, seals and dolphins shows put on at this zoo near Puerto de la Cruz are guaranteed to keep the kids entertained.

▸ P.79 ▸ PUERTO DE LA CRUZ ▸

Views

Great **views** are easy to come by on Tenerife and La Gomera. The natural diversity of the islands makes for stunning panoramas, from towering **sea cliffs** rising hundreds of metres above the waves, to **leafy valleys** containing the last remnants of ancient forests. The human impact on the land, meanwhile, has left a number of well preserved **picturesque towns** and villages, providing visitors with plenty of photo opportunities.

Acantilados de Los Gigantes

Best appreciated from the ocean, these lava-formed cliffs stand hundreds of metres above the water.

▶ P.101 ▶ THE WEST COAST ▲

Teide from Garajonay

The trek to La Gomera's highest point is rewarded with a view looking across the ocean to Tenerife's highest point, Teide.

▶ P.157 ▶ NORTHERN LA GOMERA ▲

Garachico

Head up to the Mirador de Garachico viewpoint for a perfect view of this picturesque town.

▸ P.90 ▸ GARACHICO ▲

View of San Sebastián

A steep climb from the east side of La Gomera's capital is rewarded with views over the town, its long sandy beach and sparkling marina.

▸ P.139 ▸ SAN SEBASTIÁN ▸

La Orotava's rooftops

La Orotava's steep slopes allow wonderful views across the town's sixteenth-century rooftops.

▸ P.85 ▸ LA OROTAVA ◂

Beaches

Tenerife and La Gomera have few natural beaches along their rocky coastlines, but to satisfy the tourist appetite, a few have been made on Tenerife using imported sand from the Sahara. The beaches of the popular southern resorts, **Las Américas** and **Los Cristianos**, tend to be crowded affairs offering various water sports, though quieter, more secluded options are easy to find across both islands.

Playa de las Teresitas

Northeast of Santa Cruz, this is the best sand beach on the island – and surprisingly quiet outside summer weekends.

▸ P.66 ▸ THE ANAGA ▲

El Médano

Easily the best natural beach on Tenerife, though strong winds sometimes make a windbreak a necessity.

▸ P.124 ▸ THE SOUTH COAST ▲

Playa Bollullo

Idyllic beach at the base of some cliffs, an enjoyable half-day hike from Puerto de la Cruz.

▸ P.79 ▸ PUERTO DE LA CRUZ   ▲

Playa Jardin

Puerto's main beach is rarely crowded and the promenade running alongside is lined with cafés and bars.

▸ P.78 ▸ PUERTO DE LA CRUZ   ▸

Playa Fañabé

Touristy but decent beach, with plenty of bars and restaurants nearby.

▸ P.112 ▸ LOS CRISTIANOS, LAS AMÉRICAS AND COSTA ADEJE ◂

Playa de las Vistas

This huge sweep of sand between Los Cristianos and Las Américas is the best in the area and rarely over-crowded.

▸ P.110 ▸ LOS CRISTIANOS, LAS AMÉRICAS AND COSTA ADEJE ▾

Watersports

Messing about in the water is a favourite pastime for both locals and holidaymakers on Tenerife. As you'd expect from an island with reliably good weather, there are plenty of options to suit every pocket and interest, though bear in mind that water temperatures tend to be cool year-round, so wetsuits are the norm.

Jetskiing

For a bit of high-speed water fun, the Costa Adeje is the place to try your hand at jetskiing.

▶ P.112 ▶ LOS CRISTIANOS, LAS AMÉRICAS AND COSTA ADEJE ▲

Diving

Good visibility, plenty of fish and a few wrecks make the coastal waters of Tenerife and La Gomera an excellent choice for experienced divers. Novices can take courses.

▶ P.170 ▶ ESSENTIALS ▲

Snorkelling

Sheltered bays suitable for snorkelling can be found in many places on both Tenerife and La Gomera.

▶ P.170 ▶ ESSENTIALS ▼

Sailing

Follow in the wake of Colombus, with a sailing trip in the Gomera Channel.

▶ P.171 ▶ ESSENTIALS ▲

Windsurfing and kitesurfing

The coast around El Médano is internationally renowned for its excellent conditions, bringing international competitions here regularly.

▶ P.170 ▶ THE SOUTH COAST ▶

Surfing

Tenerife attracts surfers and bodyboarders keen to test their skills against the large Atlantic rollers. Beginners are best starting out in Las Américas.

▶ P.170 ▶ ESSENTIALS ▼

Hikes in Tenerife and La Gomera

With incredibly varied terrain, impressive landscapes and unique ecologies, Tenerife and La Gomera make great year-round **hiking** destinations. On **Tenerife**, the Parque Nacional del Teide is the obvious place to head, though well-marked hikes also include the rugged Anaga and Teno regions and the densely forested Orotava Valley. **La Gomera's** most enticing areas are among the ancient laurel forest of the Parque Nacional de Garajonay but, again, you can find first-class hiking along almost any of the island's steep sided gorges. The times we give for hikes indicate the difficulty of terrain that distances can't convey.

Anaga

Rugged and undeveloped, the Anaga region is the serious hiker's idea of heaven.

▸ P.66 ▸ THE ANAGA ▲

Paisaje Lunar

This extraordinary lunar landscape in the midst of majestic Canarian pine forest has some great trails running through it.

▸ P.129 ▸ MOUNT TEIDE AND
THE INTERIOR ▲

Cumbre de Chijeré

To see first-hand why the "beautiful valley" of Vallehermoso is so called, all you need do is follow this ridge walk.

▶ P.161 ▶ NORTHERN LA GOMERA ▲

Garajonay

Hiking up La Gomera's highest mountain takes you through ancient laurel trees and offers views over four neighbouring islands.

▶ P.157 ▶ NORTHERN LA GOMERA ▼

La Catedrál

A hike around Los Roques de García allows a closer look at the weird rock formations in this area, including La Catedrál.

▶ P.134 ▶ MOUNT TEIDE AND THE INTERIOR ▲

Barranco de Masca

Hiking and scrambling down this gorge is a unique and awe-inspiring experience – but strictly for the fit.

▶ P.100 ▶ THE TENO ▼

Places

Places

Santa Cruz

The dynamic city of Santa Cruz is where the Spanish conquest of Tenerife began – it was here that Alfonso de Lugo planted his holy cross in 1494 before heading inland to found the island's first town, La Laguna. The government moved from La Laguna to the flourishing port of Santa Cruz in 1723 where it has remained since, and though the city is no aesthete's delight, its uniquely Canarian urban vibrance is worth experiencing. The seafront Plaza de España – and its controversial memorial to the 39 soldiers from the island who fought for Franco and the fascists in the civil war – forms the central focus for the city and adjoins Plaza Candelaria which is lined with cafes and shops. The main pedestrian drag, Calle de Castillo, extends west from here and Santa Cruz's few sights are scattered in the streets either side of here and along the seafront.

Museo de Bellas Artes

C/José Murphy 4. Mon–Fri 10am–7pm. Free. Though it also holds an eclectic mix of weapons, coins and sculptures – including a Rodin – the Museo de Bellas Artes (Fine Art Museum) concentrates mainly on paintings. There's a good selection of Canarian artists on display, plus nineteenth-century landscapes along with some battlefields and religious depictions by old masters such as van Loo and Brueghel.

Centro de Arte la Recova

Plaza Isla de la Madera ☎922 29 07 35. Mon–Sat 11am–1pm & 6–9pm. Free. Sometimes referred to as the Centro de Fotografía, the Centro de Arte la Recova is a modern art and photography museum with frequently changing, often experimental and generally engaging exhibitions of little known artists and photographers.

Iglesia de Nuestra Señora de la Concepción

Plaza Concepción. Mass Mon–Sat 9am & 7.30pm; Sun & church holidays 9am, 11am, noon, 1pm, 6pm & 8pm with entry 30min before. Begun in 1502 and taking over two centuries to complete, the Iglesia de Nuestra Señora de la Concepción is

Arrival and information

Santa Cruz's **bus station** is south of the centre, around ten-minutes' walk from the seafront Plaza de España; buses arrive here from almost every corner of the island. Arriving by car head here too (follow signs for the Avda. Maritima), and leave the car in the underground car park below the plaza. The town's **tourist office** (Mon–Fri 9am–4pm, Sat 9am–1pm; ☎922 23 95 92), on the western side of the Plaza de España, supplies free town maps and has some information on the rest of the island.

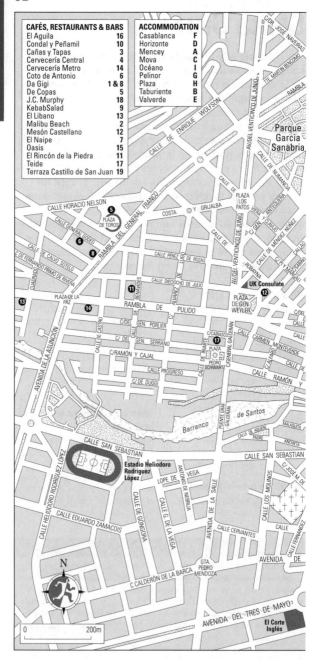

CAFÉS, RESTAURANTS & BARS	
El Aguila	16
Condal y Peñamil	10
Cañas y Tapas	3
Cervecería Central	4
Cervecería Metro	14
Coto de Antonio	6
Da Gigi	1 & 8
De Copas	5
J.C. Murphy	18
KebabSalad	9
El Libano	13
Malibu Beach	2
Mesón Castellano	12
El Naipe	7
Oasis	15
El Rincón de la Piedra	11
Teide	17
Terraza Castillo de San Juan	19

ACCOMMODATION	
Casablanca	F
Horizonte	D
Mencey	A
Mova	C
Océano	I
Pelinor	G
Plaza	H
Taburiente	B
Valverde	E

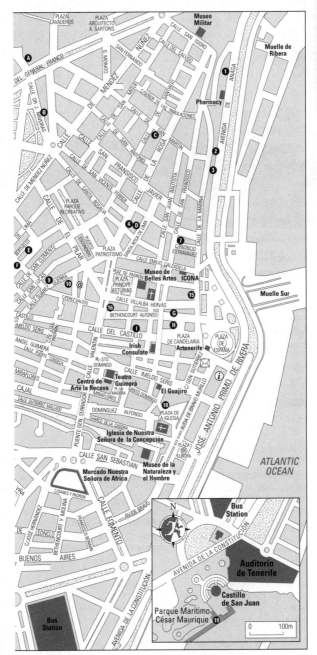

▲ IGLESIA DE NUESTRA SEÑORA DE LA CONCEPCIÓN

Santa Cruz's oldest and most important church and a handy landmark thanks to its tall belltower. The building has been gutted by fire several times, meaning that what remains today dates mostly from the seventeenth and eighteenth centuries. Relics and articles of historic significance kept here include part of the *Santa Cruz de la conquista* (Holy Cross of the Conquest), which dominates the silver Baroque main altar and gave the city its name.

Museo de la Naturaleza y el Hombre

C/Fuentes Moreales ☎922 20 93 20, ⊕www.cabtfe.es. Tues–Sun 9am–8.30pm. €1.50. Housed in an eighteenth-century, former hospital building, the city's premier museum, the Museo de la Naturaleza y el Hombre (Museum of Nature and Man) contains informative and well-constructed displays on Canarian natural history and archeology. The most fascinating exhibits relate to the Guanches with examples of their pottery, tools and rock art all displayed

here, though most memorable are the gruesome mummified bodies and collection of skeletons.

Museo Militar

C/San Isidro 2 ☎922 34 85 00. Tues–Sun 10am–2pm. Free. Santa Cruz's Museo Militar (Military Museum) has exhibitions on the evolution of weaponry through the ages, but largely focuses on the town's finest military hour – its repulse of the attack by Lord Nelson in 1797 in which the seafaring hero lost not only many of his men, but, more famously, his right arm. The cannon "El Tigre", that allegedly blew off the limb, is on display, as are captured flags.

Auditorio de Tenerife

Avda. de la Constitución ⊕www.auditoriodetenerife.com. Looking like a huge wave, the new, immense and head-turning Auditorio provides Santa Cruz with a first-class venue for the arts. The building cleverly plays on a nautical theme, with many of its windows shaped like portholes and the tiny tiles on its bright white exterior shimmering like fish scales. For a glimpse inside you'll have to attend a performance (see p.60).

Castillo de San Juan

Avda. de la Constitución. The Castillo de San Juan makes a striking contrast with its neighbour, the Auditorio. This dark stout little seventeenth-century portside fort once guarded the town's harbour and was also the site of a bustling trade in African slaves, but unfortunately it's not open to visitors.

Parque Marítimo

Avda. de la Constitución ☎ 922 20 32 44. Mon–Sat 11am–6pm, Sun 10am–6pm. €1.50. In the absence of a city beach, the Parque Marítimo is where Santa Cruz's inhabitants come to take a dip in one of the sea-water pools or soak up the sun and the views along the coast. The complex was designed by Canarian artist César Manrique – in the same style as the more famous lido in Puerto de la Cruz (see p.78) –

and includes, apart from the pools, shops, fountains, a restaurant and a sauna.

Hotels

Horizonte

C/Santa Rosa de Lima 11 ☎ & ℱ 922 27 19 36. Inexpensive hotel on the edge of the central pedestrian area with worn and dated decor, but large en-suite rooms and some good-value singles. €35.

Mencey

C/Doctor José Naveiras 38 ☎ 922 27 67 00, ⊛ www.luxurycollection.com /mencey. Swanky, 286-room palace whose architecture is inspired by 1920s casino hotels. Rooms have plush antique furnishings and facilities include a pool and tennis courts in the palm garden, plus a ritzy casino open to non-residents (daily 9pm–5am). €200.

Océano

C/Castillo 6 ☎ 922 27 08 00. Good-value hotel, above the shops of the town's main pedestrian

▼ AUDITORIO DE TENERIFE

street. The functional rooms are cramped, but rather grandly appointed with a surfeit of marble. Room rates include breakfast. €48.

Pelinor

C/Béthencourt Alfonso 8 ☎922 24 68 75, ☏922 28 05 20. Large, airy rooms in a labyrinthine hotel complex right in the centre. Though the straightforward rooms are in a good state of repair, the hotel as a whole has a slightly rundown feel – but it's clean throughout and prices include breakfast. €50.

Plaza

Plaza Candelaria 10 ☎922 27 24 53, ☏922 27 51 60. Well-run hotel with plain but comfortable rooms. At weekends there are good-value two-night offers, and its singles are the best value in town. Price includes a breakfast buffet. €60.

Taburiente

C/Dr José Naveirs 24A ☎922 27 60 00, ☏hotabu@teleline.es. Grand, modern hotel with reasonable prices. All rooms are en suite and have TV and fridge, and many overlook the Parque García Sanabria. Communal facilities include a roof terrace with small pool, a Jacuzzi and a sauna. €67.

Pensions

Casablanca

C/Viera y Clavijo 15 ☎922 27 85 99. None-too-clean pension with mostly windowless rooms and shared bathrooms, whose redeeming feature is its excellent downtown location and small roof terrace that creates a sociable vibe lacking elsewhere. Some smarter rooms and singles are available. €15.

Mova

C/San Martin 33 ☎922 28 32 61. The pick of the low-budget pensions, with clean singles and doubles available (with or without private baths) in a slightly rundown part of town that's nevertheless handy for the nightlife along Avenida Anaga. The owners speak some English. €24–36.

Valverde

C/Sabino Berthelot 46 ☎922 27 40 63. Well-turned-out but not very friendly pension above a bar on a centrally located pedestrian street. Some rooms have private bathrooms. €12–24.

▼ PLAZA CANDELARIA

▲ MERCADO NUESTRA SEÑORA DE AFRICA

Shops

Artenerife

Plaza de España ☎ 922 29 15 23.
Mon–Fri 10am–1.30pm & 4–7pm, Sat
10am–1pm. One of a chain of
small shops in all the major
towns of the island, selling high-
quality handicrafts made in
Tenerife – mostly pottery, lace
and woodwork.

El Corte Inglés

Avda. Tres de Mayo. Mon–Sat
10am–10pm Comprehensive
department store where the
emphasis is on high-quality
products and first-class service.
The café at the top has great
views of the harbour and
makes an ideal break from
shopping.

El Guajiro

C/Imeldo Seris 15. Mon–Fri 9am–1pm
& 5–8pm; Sat 9am–1pm. Small, old-
fashioned tobacconist where
cigars are packed by hand and a
good range of smoking
paraphernalia is on sale. A
similar shop is on the same
street at no. 23.

Mercado Nuestra Señora de Africa

C/San Sebastián. Daily early to 1pm.
Large multi-level covered
market in simple but elegant
Moorish buildings. Great for
groceries and deli items at
reasonable prices – look out
particularly for local cheeses like
the salty and deliciously light
queso fresco. Just outside, the
Sunday-morning flea market is a
great place for unusual
souvenirs.

Cafés

El Aguila

Plaza Alféreces Provisionales. With
lots of outdoor seating beside an
elegant dragon tree and the lush
Plaza Príncipe de Asturias, this
café is a popular meeting place
and a better bet than the more
obvious but bland and relatively
pricey choices lining Plaza
Candelaria.

Condal y Peñamil

Callejón del Combate 9–13 ☎ 922 24
90 58. The selection of

newspapers and extensive range of coffees and cigars encourage lingering in this gloriously old-world café with polished brass, dark wood, maroon drapes and suave service. Seating is either inside or in a small pedestrian alley.

Oasis

C/de la Marina 19b. Closed Wed. Basic little strip-lit café with a range of excellent cheap Italian ice creams and sinful cakes.

Restaurants

Cañas y Tapas

Avda. Anaga 15. Branch of the moderately expensive restaurant chain with dark wood and tile decor and some outside seating. A large selection of tapas includes blood sausage, a salami platter and octopus. Vegetarians will find quite a few options too.

Cervecería Central

C/Santa Rosalia 47. Daily 8am–2am. With a pleasant plaza-side location, this large restaurant is a good option for lunch, offering a fair selection of reasonably priced tapas, sandwiches, omelettes and *revueltos* (scrambled-egg dishes) plus an acceptable gazpacho. More substantial meals are provided by a predictable range of local fish and meat dishes.

Coto de Antonio

C/General Goded 13 ☎922 27 21 05. Closed Sun & Aug. Elegant, simply decorated place, consistently popular with locals and visitors alike. The excellent menu is based around Basque and Canarian cuisine, with superb and varied – though pricey – daily dishes as well as regular favourites including roast kid.

Da Gigi

Avda. Anaga 43 ☎922 28 46 07 and Rambla General Franco 27 ☎922 27 43 26. Italian restaurant, with two outlets, each with stylish brick interiors and located in the city's most popular dining areas. The menu features a good selection of *antipasta*, an excellent range of fresh pastas and a large selection of fantastic thin-crust pizzas – all moderately priced.

KebabSalad

C/Suárez Guerra 31. Daily 11am–11pm. Bright little self-service place that's the best budget option in town. Here €6 gets you a kebab, a trip to the fantastic salad bar and a canned drink.

El Libano

C/Santiago Cuadrado 36 ☎922 28 59 14. Daily 8pm–late. Simple Lebanese restaurant tucked in a side street and offering old favourites such as kebabs and stuffed vine leaves at reasonable prices, along with more unusual dishes such as *beme* – a traditional vegetable dish – and a superb selection of vegetarian options.

Mesón Castellano

C/Lima 4 ☎922 27 10 74. Closed Sun. Daily 1–4pm & 8pm–midnight. Atmospheric basement restaurant serving expensive fish and meat dishes and specializing in a range of sausage-based dishes. The rustic little bar on the ground floor above the restaurant is a pleasant place for a quiet drink.

El Rincón de la Piedra

C/Benavides 32 ☎922 24 97 78. Closed Thurs. Cavernous and beautiful old house with restored woodwork, beamed ceilings and a friendly atmosphere. The expensive food includes a good range of salads and some fish, but the restaurant is best known for its meat dishes, including a superb *solomillo*.

Teide

C/Cairasco 13. No-nonsense strip-lit bar with plastic tables, football on TV and a selection of four daily menus of reasonable quality for €5.40 including a drink.

▲ PLAZA DE ESPAÑA

Bars

Cervecería Metro

Rambla de Pubido 89. Dingy pub-style place with a huge range of European beers and a varied crowd, close to the Plaza de la Paz in an area that's something of a focus for bars. For alternative watering holes check the unnamed passage opposite.

J.C. Murphy

Plaza de Iglesia. Daily 5pm–2am. Classy Irish pub that's great for a quiet drink among thirtysomethings in an upcoming area of bars and restaurants around the Iglesia de la Concepción.

Terraza Castillo de San Juan

Avda. de la Constitución. June–Sept generally Thurs–Sun 10pm–5am. Outdoor bar with spectacular setting beside the Auditoro and Castillo de San Juan. During the summer months this and other *terrazas* largely eclipse local indoor venues.

Clubs

De Copas

C/Horacio Nelson 11. Open until 5am. Though some distance from other nightspots, this enjoyable club, with fabulous gardens and two dance-floors – one with Latin music, the other hip-hop or chart – is worth the trek.

Malibu Beach

Avda. Anaga 31. Thurs–Sun 11pm–3.30am. Lively, surfing-theme club that's a popular option among the many trendy bars and clubs that line the town's main nightlife strip Avenida de Anaga. None get going until midnight, but most pump out chart music until around 5am.

El Naipe

C/Patricio Estevanez 6. 10pm–3am. Simple little salsa bar with a great Latin vibe, where everyone's having a good time and novices on the dance floor are happily tolerated.

Live music

Auditorio de Tenerife

Avda. de la Constitución ☎922 27 06 11, ⊛www.auditoriodetenerife.com. This eye-catching venue for the performing arts (see p.54) has great acoustics and is home to Tenerife's well-respected symphony orchestra. The Festival de Música de Canarias in February is the highlight of the annual calendar.

Teatro Guimerá

C/Imeldo Seris ☎922 29 08 38. Imposing Classical building with elaborate stuccowork that's Tenerife's longest-standing performing arts venue. Its programme includes classical music, ballet, opera and theatre performances.

▲ TEATRO GUIMERÁ

La Laguna

A good deal higher than Santa Cruz and so with a considerably cooler and rainier climate, the lively university town of **La Laguna** was Tenerife's first major settlement and, for over two hundred years, its capital. The government may have moved and the town's bland suburbs now blur into Santa Cruz, yet La Laguna remains the cultural, religious and academic centre of Tenerife and its well-preserved historic centre provides a showpiece of Canarian architecture. South of here, it's the university district that is the busiest area of town, its streets buzzing with bars, cafés and bookshops.

La Laguna is at its best during festivals, particularly Corpus Christi, when many of its central streets are bedecked with detailed patterns of flowers.

Plaza del Adelantado

Leafy Plaza del Adelantado is at the heart of the historic centre and contains the *ayuntamiento* (town hall) and the Convento Santa Catalina, built in 1611, whose wooden grill on the upper floor allowed the nuns to watch events in the square below without being seen. Focal point of the plaza is a statue of Friar Anchieta, who was born in the town and later emigrated to South America, where he is said to have converted over two million local people to Christianity.

▲ PLAZA DEL ADELANTADO

Arrival and information

Buses #14 and #15 from Santa Cruz (very frequent, 25–40min) run to La Laguna's **bus station**, a ten-minute walk west of the centre: head along Calle Manuel Hernandez Martín. If arriving by car, park on the outskirts and walk in as it's difficult to find a space in the centre.

A small **tourist information** kiosk (Mon–Sat 9am–7pm) on Plaza del Adelantado provides a list of accommodation, town maps and a couple of glossy brochures on local architecture (in Spanish).

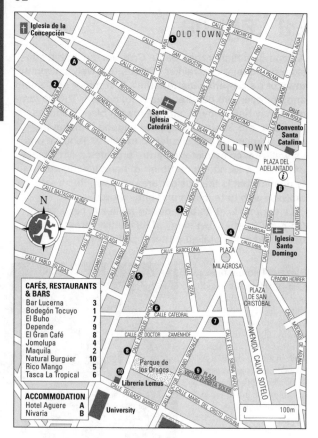

Map legend:

† Iglesia de la Concepción

OLD TOWN

Santa Iglesia Catedrál

Convento Santa Catalina

PLAZA DEL ADELANTADO ℹ

Iglesia Santo Domingo

PLAZA MILAGROSA

PLAZA DE SAN CRISTÓBAL

N

Parque de los Dragos

Librería Lemus

University

CAFÉS, RESTAURANTS & BARS

Bar Lucerna	3
Bodegón Tocuyo	1
El Buho	7
Depende	9
El Gran Café	8
Jomolupa	4
Maquila	2
Natural Burguer	10
Rico Mango	5
Tasca La Tropical	6

ACCOMMODATION

Hotel Aguere	A
Nivaria	B

0 — 100m

Museo de la Historia de Tenerife

C/San Agustín ☎922 82 59 43.
Tues–Sun 10am–8pm. €4. In a line
of sixteenth-century houses, the
Museo de la Historia de
Tenerife occupies the beautifully
restored former home of the
wealthy Lecaro family –
Genoese merchants,
moneylenders and speculators,
who, having made their fortune
running mercantile operations
on spice routes through Asia,
became one of Tenerife's most
powerful families. The house is
worth a look in its own right
but there are also exhibits
containing numerous
documents, maps and artefacts
relating to the town's history
and that of the Lecaro family.

Santa Iglesia Catedral

Plaza de la Catedral. Mon–Sat
10.30am–1.30pm & 5.30–7pm. The
town's largest church and
technically the religious centre
of Tenerife, the Santa Iglesia
Catedral was only consecrated
in 1913. Its exterior is rather
drab, while the interior is a

more impressive mixture of Baroque and Gothic, the latter seen clearly in the pointed arches of the presbytery and in the decorated windows of the east end. The cathedral treasury contains the figures that head the Christmas, Easter and Corpus Christi processions and behind the ornate altar is the tomb of Alonso de Lugo, conqueror of the islands, who died in 1525.

Iglesia de la Concepción

Plaza de la Concepción. Daily 10.30am–12.30pm. As the island's first major town and religious centre, La Laguna has several grand and impressive churches reflecting its former status. The oldest of these, and in fact the island's first, is the Iglesia de la Concepción, northwest of the cathedral, which has evolved over the years in a number of different styles of which Gothic is most evident. The green-glazed baptism pool, an original fitting in the church, was once the scene of many Guanche christenings. The church's impressive ceiling collapsed in 1972, but its replacement – a coffered *Mudéjar* affair with a complex geometric design – is, if anything, even more splendid.

▲ IGLESIA DE LA CONCEPCIÓN

Nivaria

Plaza del Adelantado 11 ☎922 26 42 98, ⊕922 25 96 34. A restored eighteenth-century house, overlooking the town's main plaza, with small, simply decorated apartments. The complex also contains a squash court and a bar. €70.

Hotels

Aguere

C/Obispo Rey Redondo 57 ☎922 25 94 90, ⊕922 63 16 33. Stylish old hotel whose uncluttered rooms surround a pretty central courtyard. Singles are available and prices include breakfast. €60.

Shops

Librería Lemus

C/Heraclio Sánchez 64 ☎922 25 11 45. Easily Tenerife's best bookshop, this place has an extensive range of titles – including a useful local travel section – though most are in Spanish.

Cafés

El Gran Café

C/Heraclio Sánchez 50. Trendy, inexpensive café, aimed at students, offering snacks and tapas. In the evenings it becomes an unpretentious and sociable place to sit, drink and smoke.

Restaurants

Bar Lucerna

C/Heraclio Sánchez 10. Inexpensive, brightly lit bar with predictable bar food but a great selection of fish and meat dishes. Good value menu of the day, delicious potato and lentil soup and a fine range of fruit juices too.

Maquila

Callejón Maquila ☎922 25 70 20. Closed Tues & Aug. In business for over a hundred years, this is the best restaurant in town. The decor is rustic and simple, as are many of the dishes, such as rabbit and goat in spicy sauces

and oven-baked lamb. The stuffed squid is the house speciality. In light of the quality, prices are very reasonable.

Natural Burguer

C/Heraclio Sanchez 58. One of many bars and bistros on this street, this hip burger joint courts students with a varied, cheap and surprisingly healthy menu that includes veggie options.

Rico Mango

Avda. de la Trinidad 47. Open 1–4pm & 7.30–11.30pm. Closed Sun. Vegetarian restaurant with great, reasonably priced South American cooking and somewhat Bohemian decor – customers visit Mars or Venus toilets.

Tasca La Tropical

Corner of C/Heraclio Sánchez & C/Catedral. This place has a good selection of snacks and moderately priced meals including a huge range of excellent *revuelto* (scrambled egg) dishes.

▼ STREET IN THE OLD TOWN

Bars

Bodegón Tocuyo

C/Juan de Vera 16. Daily noon–3pm &
7pm–2am. Dingy, darkwood pub,
covered in graffiti and with
barrels for tables, this is easily
the town's most atmospheric bar
for a quiet drink. The cheese
and meat platter is a good
accompaniment.

Depende

Plaza Victor Zurbita Soler local 11–12
☎922 25 44 42. One of the more
stylish of a number of studenty
bars lining Calle del Doctor
Antonio González and the
adjacent Plaza Victor Zurbita
Soler. This place also has a
variety of board games to play.

Clubs

Jomolupa

Plaza Milagrosa. Thurs–Sun
11pm–late. Late-night basement
club that's reliably busy once
everywhere else has shut; music
can vary between hip-hop and
salsa. No cover charge.

Live Music

El Buho

C/Catedral 3. Daily 6pm–late. One of
La Laguna's few dependable live-
music venues which calls itself a
chillout jazz bar, though you're
just as likely to hear rock. For
gig details look out for posters
along Calle del Doctor Antonio.

The Anaga

Geologically the oldest part of the island, the volcanic **Anaga** range is a rugged jumble of knife-edge ridges and deep valleys that offers some of Tenerife's most spectacular hiking. One sinuous main road runs along the length of the range, following its central ridge through upland areas smothered in the last remnant of a forest that dominated the Mediterranean until ice ages restricted it to the Canary Islands. To the north of the road, the coastline is dotted with small pebble beaches, while to the south lie two fine stretches of sand – Playa

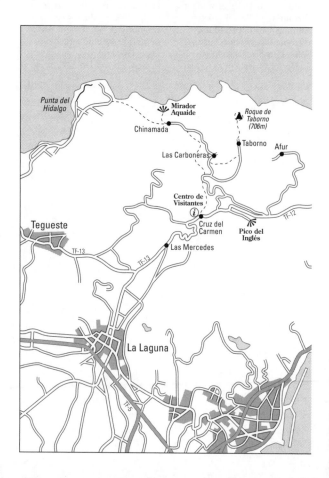

de las Teresitas and the quieter Playa de las Gaviotas. Small communities have survived in isolated hamlets in this remote region but there's little in the way of services, meaning the area is best explored on long day-trips from Santa Cruz.

Playa de las Teresitas and Playa de las Gaviotas

Buses #910, #245 & #246 from Santa Cruz, frequent, 20min. Below the leafy hillside village of San Andrés, the large artificial Playa de las Teresitas was built to provide Santa Cruz with a beach escape beside the towering Anaga mountains. A large man-made breakwater eliminates waves and currents around the palm-studded sand, and good facilities make it a pleasant place for a day of sunbathing.

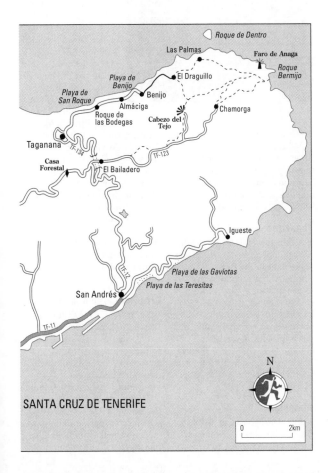

▲ PLAYA DE LAS TERESITAS

useful point of access for **Playa del San Roque** and **Playa de Benijo**, both of which are popular with local surfers – high winds along this coast can make for awe-inspiring breakers – and have a few bars and restaurants.

Benijo and El Draguillo hike

The sealed road from Almáciga ends at the tiny village of Benijo. From here a dirt road continues 2km east along the coast to the village of El Draguillo – so called for its dragon tree – where the path splits. The coastal trail (a 6km return hike) heads east to the **Faro de Anaga** lighthouse via the scenic village of Las Palmas and within sight of the bird reserve Roque de Dentro, while the route heading inland climbs steeply to Chamorga (see p.70). The two can be made into an 11-kilometre loop; if you do this, it's best to head in an anti-clockwise direction first to get all the climbing out of the way early on.

Cruz del Carmen hike

Bus #73, #75, #76 or #77 from La Laguna, 10–15 daily, 25min. Cruz del Carmen is a good gateway to the region as it's easily accessed by bus, though there's not much here save a viewpoint, a basic restaurant and a visitors' centre (Tues–Sun 9am–3pm; ☎922 63 35 76), which can supply a hiking map.

A good walk from here (2hr one way), with excellent views

Playa de las Gaviotas (bus #245 only), the next cove east after Las Teresitas, is named after the seagulls that frequent it and is a much quieter stretch, popular with nudists. A bar on the front serves snacks.

Taganana

Bus #246 from Santa Cruz, 6–8 daily, 45min. Though by far the largest settlement in the Anaga, Taganana is a tiny town that began as a sugar cane centre before moving into wine production. Precariously sprawled over several ridges and steep hillsides, it was long remote from the rest of Tenerife and is worth a quick stroll for its narrow streets lined with simple old Canarian houses.

Almáciga

Bus #246 from Santa Cruz, 6–8 daily, 50min. Almáciga – terminus of the bus from Santa Cruz – is a

from the outset, leads 3km north, past the village of Las Carboneras, to the hamlet of Chinamada. If you do this as a loop, consider hiking back along the quiet road from Chinamada to Las Carboneras before either heading back to Cruz del Carmen the way you came, or extending the hike to Taborno, the village on the opposite side of the valley, where you can walk around the imposing volcanic rock monolith, the **Roque de Taborno**. This adds another two to three hours to the hike.

Chinamada

Known for its houses built in natural caves in the rock, the hamlet of Chinamada has some of the most spectacular views in the region. The panorama from the **Mirador Aguaide** just beyond the village (accessed via an obvious track beside the town plaza) is particularly dizzying. From here you can head down to the unattractive and sleepy town of Punta del Hidalgo (approx. 3hr) to catch buses back to Santa Cruz (#105; 36 daily, 1hr 10min). This route can also be done in reverse – though it's all climbing – to Cruz del Carmen (around 5hr).

El Bailadero and Mirador Cabezo del Tejo hike

Bus #77 from La Laguna, 2 daily, 50min; and #246 or #247 from Santa Cruz, 9 daily, 45min. For a long hike with stunning views across the rugged northern coast, get off bus #77 or #247 – or park the car – at the viewpoint of El Bailadero. On bus #246, get off at Cruce El Bailadero and follow a path opposite up to the viewpoint. From here, you can walk in a loop to Almáciga (approx 10km; 4–5hr, see opposite) and catch the bus back to Santa Cruz. The walk heads east from the viewpoint along the road to Chamorga for just over a kilometre before turning onto a track signposted El Pijara. This passes through prime laurel forest and joins then leaves the road before you eventually come to the Mirador Cabezo del Tejo with superb views across the whole north side of the Anaga range. A little further along from the

▼ TAGANANA

viewpoint, the path comes to a crossroads where you turn left to head down to El Draguillo and from there to Almáciga (see p.68), right to Chamorga (6km/3hr hike from El Bailadero; see p.69), or straight on to Roque Bermijo (4km/2hr; see below).

Chamorga

Bus #247 from Santa Cruz, 3 daily, 1hr 10min. Chamorga is a small, well-kept village spread across a valley that's studded with palms and dotted with neat terraces. The village is an easy day-trip from Santa Cruz and gives access to some of the best walks in the region. One good **hike** (7km/3hr) follows a loop from Chamorga east down the valley to a small cluster of houses near **Roque Bermijo**, a sharp spit of land in the sea. From here

you climb back to Chamorga by way of a well-graded ridge walk that starts near the Faro de Anaga lighthouse. For a longer loop (14km/7hr) hike north to El Draguillo and then east along the remote coastal path to the lighthouse (see p.68) before completing the loop to Chamorga via either the valley or ridge.

Restaurants

Bar La Caseta de Pastora El Frontón

Benijo ☎922 59 01 07. Closed Mon. Great place for simple, moderately priced Canarian food, at the end of the tarmac road in Benijo. The views over the coast are tremendous.

Bar El Petón

Behind Castillo de San Andrés, San Andrés. Tucked away behind the old fort, this excellent, inexpensive seafood place stays open until the day's catch has been served. Not as good local fish and seafood places line the seafront.

La Gran Paella

C/Pedro Schwartz 15, San Andrés. Closed Tues. Simple but elegant restaurant behind the ruined Castillo de San Andrés. The paella is fantastic and unusually there's a large number of sauces to accompany the seafood.

José Cañón

Afúr ☎922 69 01 41. Closed Mon. Rustic place in the centre of tiny Afúr, with basic food cooked in vast pots and served with the minimum of fuss. Best place on the island for upland food such as goat or rabbit and chickpeas.

▼LAUREL FOREST

Candelaria and Güímar

Though easily bypassed on the main TF-1 motorway from Santa Cruz to the southern resorts, the barren landscape of Tenerife's east coast does contain two outstanding attractions – the **Basilica at Candelaria**, considered the holiest site in the Canary Islands, and **the Pirámides of Güímar**, which predate the Spanish conquest and are of global archeological importance. Both are easy day trips from all the main resorts – but particularly accessible from Santa Cruz – and are offered on some bus tours. As Tenerife's Lourdes, Candelaria is well set up for a day-trip, Güímar rather less so, though the Puertito de Güímar – its coastal outpost – has a good choice of seafood restaurants.

Basilica de Nuestra Señora de Candelaria

Mon–Fri 7.30am–1pm & 3–8pm, Sat & Sun 7.30am–8pm. Buses #122 or #131 from Santa Cruz, 21 daily, 30min. Signposted from the motorway. West of Santa Cruz stretches a string of dormitory settlements that peter out around Candelaria, a largely avoidable town were it not for the Basilica de Nuestra Señora de Candelaria. Housing a famous **statue of the Virgin Mary**, the patron saint of the Canary Islands, this is the archipelago's most important religious site.

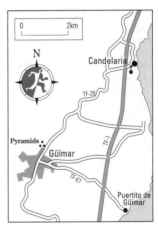

The foundation of the church was inspired by the arrival of a wooden sculpture of the Virgin (probably from the prow of a wrecked ship) washed up here in the 1390s. Initially kept in a cave and worshipped by the local Guanches, it then passed into Spanish hands after the conquest. Though the original was swept out to sea by a tidal wave in 1826, a replica, draped in silk cloth, adorned with gold and jewels and holding a baby Jesus in her arms, now forms the centrepiece of this splendid late nineteenth-century colonial-style basilica. For the Feast of the Assumption (August 15), the parading of the statue around the town attracts pilgrims from across the Canary Islands and further afield. Outside the church, the waterfront plaza is guarded by ten statues of Guanches, the work of local sculptor José Abad.

▲ BASILICA DE NUESTRA SEÑORA DE CANDELARIA

Pirámides de Güímar

☎922 51 45 10, ⓦwww
.piramidesdeguimar.net. Daily
9.30am–6pm. €9.75. Bus #121 or
124 from Santa Cruz to Güímar, 15–23
daily, 45–50min. Signposted
"pirámides". The once thriving
agricultural town of Güímar is
best known as the location of
the Pirámides de Güímar. Built
by the native Guanches, they
were long dismissed as piles of
stones heaped by farmers
clearing the land, until
archeologist Thor Heyerdahl
(famous for his Kon Tiki
voyages across the Pacific)
helped reveal their true
significance. Close inspection
revealed three pyramidal
constructions, each at least 100-
metres long and made of
carefully squared stones laid out
with considerable geometric
exactitude. The structures point
to the location of the sun
during the winter and summer
solstices and the stairs up each
flat-topped pyramid face the
rising sun. Now carefully
rebuilt to what is thought to be
their original form, a platform
and series of walkways allow

visitors to inspect the pyramids
– there's no climbing allowed.
The importance of these
structures goes far beyond an
intriguing insight into
indigenous culture and is
generally considered as
evidence of a stepping-stone in
the migration of an ancient
African culture to South
America. The site museum
focuses on this, its displays –
largely petrogylphs and pottery
– suggesting the Canaries are a
missing link between these
ancient cultures.

Hotels

Finca Salamanca

Carretera Güímar, El Puertito km1.5,
Güímar ☎922 51 45 30, ⓦwww.hotel-
fincasalamanca.com. Tranquil and
stylish country hotel, whose
collection of adobe buildings
huddles around a small pool and
is surrounded by lush gardens
and orchards. There's a stylish
restaurant too (see opposite)
where guests eat breakfast –
included in rates. €100.

Shops

La Casa de las Imagenes

Obispo Pérez Cáceres 17, Candelaria ☎922 50 21 01. Daily 10am–2pm & 4.30–8pm. One of the largest of a series of shops selling religious paraphernalia along the pedestrian road that leads to the Basilica. Choose from a bewildering array of almost invariably kitsch images, trinkets and figurines, with something for every budget.

Cafés

Carlo's

Obispo Pérez Cáceres 46, Candelaria. Tues–Sun 9.30am–9pm. Indoor café, serving a delectable assortment of ice creams. If you're not interested in sitting down, then visit the patisserie at no. 50, which has even better cakes and pastries, but no seating.

Alexia's

C/Juan P. Rodriguez Cruz 2, Puertito de Güímar. Tues–Sun 11.30am–midnight. Cheerful harbourside Venezuelan café-bar, with excellent *arepas* (maize-bread sandwiches) and *cachapas* (wheat pancakes) at around €3 each.

Restaurants

Cofrádia de Pescadores

C/Almirante Gravina 28, Puertito de Güímar. Daily May–Oct, Nov–April closed Thurs, no fixed hours. Run by the local fishermen's co-op, this is the best choice in town for fresh fish at low prices in non-fussy surroundings. If this place is closed, there are a number of other reliable options close by.

Finca Salamanca

Carretera Güímar, El Puertito km1.5, Güímar ☎922 51 45 30. 1.30–4pm & 7–10.30pm. Closed Tues. Smart hotel restaurant in an old tobacco drying room with superb and reasonably priced steaks and a phenomenal paella that requires 24-hours notice. The lobster salad is a good lunchtime choice and can be enjoyed on the shaded outdoor patio.

Casa Sindo

Obispo Pérez Cáceres 10, Candelaria ☎922 50 06 09. Daily 11am–12.30pm. Overlooking the sea, this simple restaurant has some great fresh fish – the tuna is particularly recommended – at reasonable prices.

▼ PIRÁMIDES DE GÜÍMAR

Puerto de la Cruz and around

With over a hundred years' pedigree in the field, **Puerto de la Cruz** does resort tourism well. The bustling, former harbour was historically much favoured by British traders who made the town a fashionable spa in the 1890s, and it soon became the preferred haunt for wintering European royalty and dignitaries such as Winston Churchill and Bertrand Russell. In more recent years mass tourism has created a jumble of high-rise hotels, bars and discos, yet Puerto retains some of its cosmopolitan style and flair as well as the feel of a small, friendly and busy Spanish town. Particularly popular with a more mature holidaying clientele, it boasts the highest rate of return visits of any resort in the world. The town's focal point is the café-filled **Plaza del Charco** – named after the shrimp pools that once formed here at high tide – and most of Puerto's historic buildings are found nearby. From here the pedestrian area spreads west into Ranilla, a quaint old fishing quarter, and east along the seafront and through the shopping district. There are few real sights however – Puerto's main attractions are its beaches, lido and the nearby Loro Parque zoo, or coastal walks to quiet beaches and the preserved *hacienda* of Rambla de Castro.

▼ CASA DE LA ADUANA

Casa de la Aduana

C/Las Lonjas ☎922 57 81 03. Tues–Sat 11am–1pm & 6–9pm, Sun 4–8pm. Free. Though large-scale trade is now absent from Puerto's port, a handful of small fishing boats still put in here beside the town's oldest building, the timber and plaster Casa de la Aduana. This, the former customs house, was built in 1620 and now hosts photographic exhibitions, occasionally focusing on island themes.

Arrival and information

Buses arrive at the station on C/del Pozo, on the western side of the town centre. The **tourist office** is a ten-minute walk away on the Plaza de Europa by the seafront (Mon–Fri 9am–7pm, Sat 9am–1pm; ☏922/386 000).

Iglesia de Nuestra Señora de la Peña Francia

Plaza de la Iglesia. Mass daily 8.30am, 6.30pm & 7pm. Dominating the square named after it, the seventeenth-century Iglesia de Nuestra Señora de la Peña Francia is Puerto's main church. The imposing, grey-stone building is only open to the public for mass, when it's worth sneaking in for a look at the simple interior, the fine *Mudéjar* ceiling and the Baroque retable.

Casa Iriarte

C/Iriarte. Mon–Sat 10am–7pm. This eighteenth-century house was once home to various over-achievers from the Iriarte family, including politicians, diplomats and writers. Today, its courtyard is given over to the peddling of handicrafts, with an abundance of embroidery and lace for sale. A room on the first floor calls itself the **town museum** (free) and holds a somewhat scrappy collection of photographs. The rest of the first floor is devoted to a **naval museum** (€1.50) which displays a good range of painstakingly re-created model boats from the sixteenth century onwards. Other nautical odds and ends include a copy of the last letter Nelson wrote with his right arm and the first he scrawled with his left. But the most (unintentionally) entertaining display of all here is a diorama depicting the island's conquest – dreadful life-size models of a conquistador, a priest and a Guanche prostrating himself before them.

Museo Arqueológico

C/del Lomo 9a ☏922 37 14 65. Tues–Sat 11am–1pm & 5–9pm, Sun 10am–1pm. €1, Thurs free. The former fishermen's quarter of

▼OLD FISHERMAN'S HOUSES

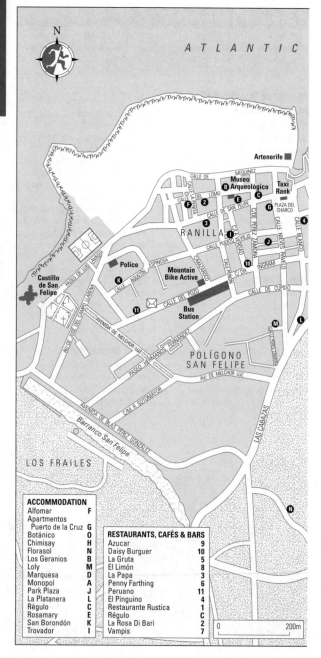

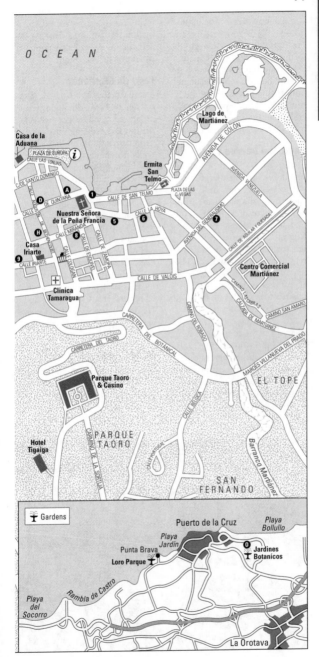

Ranilla is an area of squat, old houses and narrow roads, with the Archeological Museum on a quaint pedestrian street at its heart. The museum contains a modest collection of Guanche pottery and replicas of some mummified body parts: a collection best appreciated by specialists or on a rainy day.

Hotel and Parque Taoro

Hotel Taoro, a Puerto landmark, was the island's first large, purpose-built hotel and something of a milestone in the development of tourism. Originally constructed by an English company as a sanatorium in 1889, it was rebuilt after a fire in 1929. These days it no longer provides accommodation; instead a **casino** (daily 7.30pm–midnight; €3) and restaurant attract visitors, and there are great views over the town from its elevated position. Parque Taoro, the neat grounds surrounding the casino, contains some newer hotels, including the *Tigaiga*, a venue for **folklore shows** (Sun 11am; €2.50) that are actually more fun than they sound, including traditional dancing and singing as well as a display of Canarian wrestling.

Lago de Martiánez

Avda. Colón. Daily 8am–6pm. €3. Mats and parasols extra. Although there are several good beaches in and around Puerto, large waves and strong currents mean that it's rarely possible to bathe safely. A vast, beautifully designed open-air salt-water lido, Lago de Martiánez was built to compensate for this and successfully attracts over a million visitors a year. The complex contains a predictable array of facilities – pools, sunbathing decks, bars, cafés and changing areas – but is chiefly known for its unusual design, the work of Canarian artist César Manrique (1920–92), who added soft curves and quirky surrealist touches like the upside-down trees.

Playa Jardín

Running for almost a kilometre on the western edge of town, sandy Playa Jardín is the town's premier beach and invariably

▾ LAGO DE MARTIÁNEZ

▲ LORO PARQUE

busy. It provides all the usual facilities and the sea is sometimes calm enough for swimming, but in general the waters here are best left to experienced surfers.

Loro Parque

Punta Brava ☎922 37 38 41, ⊛www.loroparque.com. Daily 8.30am–6.45pm (last entry 5pm). €21, under-12s €10.50. Free mini-train from Avda. Venezuela. Loro Parque (Parrot Park) is Tenerife's best publicized tourist attraction. Opened in 1978, the zoo originally contained only 150 parrots, a few of which performed in a show that is still put on several times a day, and while the parrot collection now tops 1400, it's overshadowed by several more high-profile attractions. These include performances by seals and dolphins (check the timetable on entering if you plan to catch them all), some impressive aquariums (including a shark tunnel) plus gorilla and chimp enclosures. The most impressive addition, however, is the remarkable Planet Penguin, a high-tech enclosure powered by the equivalent of two thousand fridges to keep its Antarctic penguins happy at these climes.

Jardines Botánicos

Avda. Marqués Villanueva, La Paz. Daily 9am–6pm. €1.50. The subtropical Jardines Botánicos (Botanical Gardens) were originally created in 1788 by King Carlos III, who had an ambition to display species from all the Spanish colonies in his palace gardens back in Spain. He hoped Tenerife would be a good place to acclimatize the plants and he was right – but unfortunately few of the species could withstand the cooler Spanish winters leading to the ultimate failure of his tropical-garden project. With some three thousand species from around the world on display here, the variety of plants is certainly impressive, with everything from Californian palms and Brazilian shrubs growing alongside one another.

Hike to Playa Bollullo

4km/1hr 30min one-way hike. Pleasant, sandy Playa Bollullo is one of the area's best beaches – though frequently enormous waves mean that swimming is

Puerto de la Cruz and around PLACES

not usually an option. It's a good four-kilometre cliff-top hike from Puerto, starting with a steep climb up Camino Las Cabras – beside the Centro Comercial Martiánez – following the steps leading onto Camino San Amaro. Excellent views over Puerto soon open up, and the **Mirador de la Paz** viewpoint is a good place from which to enjoy them. From here you can head east along the cliff-top promenade and a rougher coastal path to Playa Bollullo, on the edge of town. A flight of steps leads down the cliff to the beach, while the path continues east to several smaller beaches where both nudism and wild camping are tolerated.

Casa del Vino La Baranda

El Sauzal ☎922 57 25 35. Tues–Sat 11am–10pm, Sun & public holidays 11am–6pm. Free. Bus #101 from Puerto de la Cruz, 21–30 daily, 40min; or Santa Cruz, 1hr to "Cruz El Sauzal" motorway junction. Casa del Vino La Baranda, Tenerife's wine

▼ CASA DEL VINO LA BARANDA

museum, is housed in a beautifully restored seventeenth-century *hacienda* in a major agricultural region, known for its fine grapes and excellent wines. Informative displays give details on the region and there's the opportunity for tastings too. If you'd like something to wash down, head to the museum's tapas bar which has excellent views over the coast, or visit its classy restaurant (see p.84).

Rambla de Castro

Bus #107, #108 & #363 from Puerto de la Cruz, 36–38 daily, 25min; or Santa Cruz, 15–17 daily, 1hr 15min to Mirador San Pedro. Occupying a picturesque headland on a stretch of coastline named after it, the Rambla de Castro estate includes a restored manor house and some fortifications at the heart of a large banana plantation. A path heads here from Puerto – follow the coastal route from the *Hotel Maritim* which lies on the coast just west of Loro Parque – and makes an excellent walk (2–3hr return), passing a ruined but grand pumphouse that once provided the *hacienda* with water from a spring. The house and fortifications can also be accessed from the main coastal road at the Mirador San Pedro.

Playa Socorro

Bus #107, #108 & #363 from Puerto de la Cruz, 36–38 daily, 27min; or Santa Cruz, 15–17 daily, 1hr 15min. This, the island's most popular natural beach, is a pleasant black-sand strip stretching a kilometre along the coast to Punta Brava and Loro Parque. It's usually overrun on summer weekends while on August evenings it attracts crowds to watch the movies projected onto massive screens – for

▲ RAMBLA DE CASTRO

details check at the tourist office or in *El Día* newspaper. In winter the sea is generally too rough for bathing, and is given over to surfers.

Hotels

Alfomar

C/Peñita 6 ☏ & ☏922 38 06 82. A small hotel housed in a 1970s building with what's now retro-chic decor. Most of the en-suite double rooms come with a balcony overlooking a quiet pedestrian street. €26.

Botánico

Urbanización El Botánico ☏922 38 14 00, ⊛www.hotelbotanico.com. A large five-star hotel, within immaculately maintained gardens to the east of town. For the price, the rooms are nothing special, though most have balconies with fine views. Facilities include restaurants, swimming pools, tennis courts and an eighteen-hole putting green. €190.

Chimisay

C/Agustín de Bethencourt 14 ☏922 38 35 52, ⊜chimisay@mx2.red.estb.es. Though it has an uninviting exterior and faded interiors, the 67 large, clean rooms here are well kept and overlook a quiet pedestrian street. There's also a small pool on the roof. €55.

Marquesa

C/Quintana 11 ☏922 38 31 51, ⊜h-marquesa@terra.es. A well established hotel in an early eighteenth-century Canarian building. Behind the ornate balconies are good modern facilities, including a reliable restaurant and a small pool. Breakfast is included in the rate. Singles available. €60.

Monopol

C/Quintana 15 ☏922 38 46 11, ⊜monopol@interbook.net. Elegant building from 1742, with wooden balconies overlooking a courtyard. The rooms are exquisitely presented, though some of the less expensive ones are rather cramped. Prices include breakfast. €55.

Régulo

C/San Felipe 6 ☏922 38 88 00, ☏922 37 04 20. Small, renovated house in the old central quarter in which the rooms facing the courtyard are significantly quieter than those facing the road. Half-board deals, with dinner at the top quality *Régulo* restaurant opposite, are around twice the price of the room-only deal. €35.

San Borondón

C/Agustín Espinosa 2 ☎922 38 33 13, ☎922 37 13 65. Group of Colonial-style buildings, just 200m from the beach and offering over a hundred rooms, a good-sized pool, tennis courts and restaurant. Prices include breakfast and dinner. €84.

Trovador

C/Puerto Viejo 38 ☎922 38 45 12, ☎922 38 45 49. Pleasant place in a central location where rooms are en suite and have balconies, TV and minibar. There's also a small pool on the roof with great sea views. Rates include a decent breakfast buffet. €80.

Pensions

La Platanera

C/Blanco 29 ☎922 38 41 57. Both single and double rooms are available in this modern house. All are en suite, and some have balconies overlooking a charming little garden. €26.

Loly

C/de la Sala 4 ☎922 38 36 93. A friendly, simple and clean pension, just outside the old town, offering double rooms with shared bath. €20.

Los Geranios

C/del Lomo 14 ☎922 38 28 10. Spotlessly clean and well-kept hotel-quality rooms (all en suite) in a friendly pension in the old fishing quarter. A basic continental breakfast is offered for a small extra charge. €27.

Rosamary

C/San Felipe 14 ☎922 38 32 53. A small, friendly and immaculately kept place, where all rooms are en suite – those with a balcony overlook a busy road and so are noisier than those without. €28.

Apartments

Apartmentos Puerto de la Cruz

CC Olympia 7, Plaza del Charco ☎922 37 37 59 or 922 38 11 24. Useful agency that can help find an apartment in town and particularly good for long-stays. Rentals start at around €200 per week for a studio.

Florasol

Camino del Coche 7 ☎922 38 98 48, ⊛www.aparthotelflorasol.com. Small complex offering well-equipped, tastefully decorated and generously sized apartments, many with views towards Teide. Facilities include a pool, tennis courts and a restaurant. €58.

Park Plaza

C/José Arroyo 2 ☎922 38 41 12, ⊛cipriang@teleline.es. A modern block of well-equipped apartments, each with a kitchen, TV and a balcony. Though tired-looking, the central location and small roof top pool compensate. €52.

Shops

Artenerife

Muelle Pesquera. Pottery, lace and carvings are some of the genuine Tenerife souvenirs available at this branch of the island-wide chain.

Centro Commercial Martiánez

C/Aguilar y Quesada. Large shopping mall in the centre of town with a range of shops and supermarkets.

▲ PUERTO'S SEAFRONT

Cafés

El Pinguino

Plaza del Charco. Daily 10am–10pm. A great spot to people-watch over one of the numerous flavours of inexpensive, home-made Italian ice-creams. Sit in and gorge on extravagant sundaes or pick up a cone to take away.

Restaurants

Azucar

C/Iriarte 1 ☎922 38 70 14. Tues–Sun 8.30pm–1am. Moderately priced Cuban food – rice-based dishes, black bean stews, fried green bananas, croquettes and tapas-like snacks – plus lively Latin American music, in a restored house in the centre of the old town.

El Caldosa

Playa Chica, Punta Brava ☎922 38 90 18. Good little restaurant off the end of Playa Jardín in Punta Brava. Superb fish and seafood at reasonable prices served in cheerful, stylish surroundings with large windows that swing open so that the waves crashing on the tiny beach can be heard.

Daisy Burguer

C/Doctor Ingram 18. Cheap and bustling burger bar, popular with the locals, and also offering omelettes and a few tapas. Open all day and well into the small hours.

El Limón

C/Esquivel and C/B.Miranda. Closed Sun lunch. Vegetarian place serving great burgers, soups, salads, sandwiches and one main dish for dinner, plus lots of fresh shakes and juices at moderate prices.

La Papa

C/San Felipe 33. Cosy restaurant with a range of Canarian food – including good thick hearty Canarian stew *Puchero* and goat dishes – and a couple of veggie options, all reasonably priced.

Peruano

C/del Pozo 18. Closed Wed & May. Decorated and named to make its Peruvian credentials quite clear, the cuisine here follows suit. Many of the inexpensive dishes are the usual local meat and seafood options with a Peruvian spin. Dried lamb sirloin is the house speciality.

Restaurante Rustica

Punta Viento. Daily noon–11pm. Not a gourmet choice, though the Italian food is tasty and inexpensive – pizzas from €5 – and the views over the coast from its cliffside location are beautiful.

La Rosa Di Bari

C/del Lomo 23 ☎922 36 85 23. Possibly the best Italian restaurant on the island, this place has oodles of panache and great – though expensive – food, including generous portions of gnocchi and pizza.

Régulo

C/Pérez Zamora 16 ☎922 38 45 06. Closed Sun & July. One of the classiest restaurants in town – with prices to match – located in a restored town house, with much of the seating in the courtyard. There's a good spread of Canarian cuisine on offer, but the place is particularly known for its seafood.

Tasca

Casa Del Vino La Baranda, El Sauzal ☎922 56 33 88. Closed Mon. Canarian fine dining option in a restored seventeenth-century *hacienda* (see p.80) with cheerful service and an exhaustive local wine list. Main courses around €10.

Bars

La Gruta

C/La Hoya 24. Grotto-themed bar that's worth a try if you'd rather settle down to some chat or live music than trawl the clubs.

Penny Farthing

C/La Hoya 32. Rather nondescript bar and disco, but a dependable favourite along pedestrian Calle La Hoya that tends to get going a bit earlier than its neighbours.

Clubs

Vampis

Edificio Drafo, Avda del Generalísimo ☎922 38 65 37. The best-known club in town, popular with transvestites, sits along the main strip of basement clubs and discos on the Avenida del Generalísimo. If you don't fancy this, there are plenty of other options nearby including, unusually for Tenerife, a few gay clubs.

La Orotava

Not only the name **La Orotava** but also the bulk of the town's original wealth comes from the prosperous, fertile green valley surrounding it. Since pre-Spanish times, this has been one of the island's most densely populated areas, and its main town blossomed as the centre of cash crop industries which still include vineyards and banana groves. Plaza de la Constitución is the busiest square in La Orotava's well-preserved old town, whose network of steep, cobbled streets is particularly known for the Doce Casas, twelve striking Canarian-style mansions that were former residences of the area's leading families. Some of these are open to the public as well-stocked handicraft shops and can, along with the town's other attractions, easily be explored on a daytrip from Puerto de la Cruz, 6km away. An ideal time to visit the town is during the celebrations of Corpus Christi, when the streets are decorated with flower petals, baked leaves and volcanic sand, a tradition begun in 1847. Another good day-trip is to head higher up **La Orotava Valley** for a spot of hiking among the Canarian pines surrounding the eye-catching rock face Los Organos.

Jardín Victoria and the Jardínes Botánicos

Daily 9am–2pm. Free. The Jardín Victoria is the nineteenth century-style garden of the Ponte family. The immaculately kept and tightly regimented layout may not be to everyone's taste, but the garden does offer great views over the coast. Just west of here are La Orotava's own tiny Jardínes Botánicos (Botanic Gardens; same hours) which include a good sized dragon tree amid a small collection of exotic plants.

▼ JARDÍN VICTORIA

Arrival and information

From La Orotava's **bus station** at the top of Avda. Jose Antonio – bus #352 and #353 from Puerto de la Cruz (35 daily, 17min) – it's a ten-minute walk west to the old town, where you'll find the **tourist office** (Mon–Fri 9am–6pm, Sat 10am–2pm; ☎922/323 041) on C/Escultor Estévez 2.

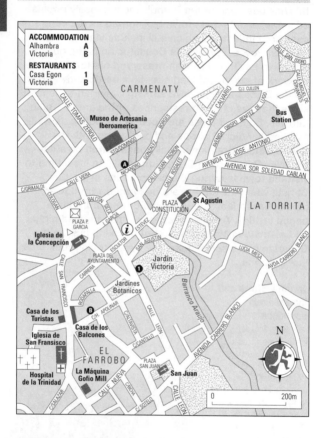

Iglesia de la Concepción

Plaza Casanas. Mass: Wed, Thurs & Fri 10am, 1pm, 5pm & 7pm; Mon 10am, 1pm, 4pm & 6pm; Sun 9am, 10am, 11.30am & 6pm. Built after the original church on this site was destroyed by earthquakes in 1704 and 1705, the Iglesia de la Concepción is a grand structure that reflects the wealth of the local community at that time. Its facade is a particularly notable piece of Baroque architecture and has been made a Spanish national monument.

Casa de Los Balcones

C/San Francisco. Mon–Sat 10am–1pm & 4–7pm. Upper levels €1.50, otherwise free. Calle de San

Francisco is known for its impressive seventeenth- and eighteenth-century mansions, the grandest of which is the Casa de Los Balcones. As its name suggests, the house is best known for is splendid, ornately worked Canarian pine balconies – facing both the street and into its pretty courtyard. The ground floor now contains a lace and linen centre, while the upper level has opulent wood-clad rooms, furnished as they would have been in the eighteenth century. A couple of adjoining rooms reconstruct the living quarters of simpler folk at this time.

▲ CASA DE LOS BALCONES

La Máquina Gofio Mill

C/San Francisco 3. Mon–Fri 8am–1pm & 2–7pm. Free. El Farrobo, the town's old mill quarter, is where the local speciality *gofio* (see p.27) has been produced for centuries. Nowadays, seven of the original *gofio* mills still survive along the phenomenally steep Calle de San Francisco, and one of them, La Máquina, still operates, albeit now with an electric motor. Photos inside depict bygone days when the quarter still clattered with the sound of the mills.

▼ OROTAVA STREET SCENE

Museo de Artesanía Iberoamericana

C/Tomás Zerolo 34 ☎922 32 17 46.
Mon–Fri 9.30am–6pm, Sat
9.30am–2pm. €2.50. Housed in the
former Convento de Santo
Domingo, the Museo de
Artesanía Iberoamericana devotes
itself to exhibiting handicrafts
and folk art from Spain and
Latin America. The beautiful old
convent building itself is as
interesting as the displays, which
focus on textiles, ceramics and
musical instruments but are
poorly explained.

La Caldera and Los Organos

Bus #345 from Puerto de la Cruz, 12
daily, 55min. Beyond the densely
settled slopes of the upper
Orotava Valley, the island's largest
pine forest takes over, nourished
by the mists that regularly
shroud these heights. The area is
crisscrossed by many paths, most
of them wide forest tracks that
can be linked to form good
hiking routes. A useful starting
point for walks in the area is La
Caldera, a picnic spot in an old
volcanic crater, 2km south of
the village of Aguamansa and

LA CALDERA & AROUND

some 6km southeast of La
Orotava. A kiosk beside the
crater also does light meals,
including fresh trout from a
local fish farm. From just past
the kiosk and signposted "Pista
Monte del Pino", it's a very easy
ten-minute walk down a flat
dirt road to view Los Organos, a
row of massive basalt pillars
moulded by crystallization into
organ-pipe shapes.

Hike around Los Organos

16km/5hr circular hike. Strenuous
but rewarding, this hike is easily
the most exhilarating walk in La
Orotava Valley, with views on
clear days stretching down to
Puerto de la Cruz. Even in poor
weather the eerie drama of
lichen-draped pine trees in the
mist is wonderfully memorable.
The route forms a loop
beginning and ending along the
"Pista Monte Del Pino".

About one kilometre from La
Caldera, bear right when you
arrive at a forest shelter onto an
uphill path signed "Pedro Gill".
It climbs steeply for around
40min – ignore a narrow track
crossing it almost halfway up –
to an area of more widely
spaced pines and a T-junction,
beyond a short section that
follows a dry stream-bed. Turn
left at this junction following a
good, simple-to-follow path that
turns slightly downhill at first for
approximately 6km (2hr). This
trail ducks in and out of a
number of dry gorges and
includes some short narrow
sections where ropes have been
attached for support. Not long
after the last of these is the easily
missed turn-off to the left,
where the trail heads past a
rocky outcrop before zigzagging
steeply downwards. The narrow
path soon joins a wider and
winding trail which you follow.

▲ ROOFTOPS IN LA OROTAVA

Keep left here, then turn right at the T-junction further down. This leads into increasingly dense and lush forest on a trail that doubles back on itself until you reach another T-juction with the Pista Monte Del Pino. A left turn here will lead you back along the dirt road to La Caldera in around 45min, passing Los Organos on your left as you reach the final stretch.

Hotels

Alhambra

C/Nicandro Gonzales Borges 19 ☎922 32 04 34, ⊛www.alhambra.teneriffa .com. Stylish and highly recommended villa with Moorish decor and sea views. There are six large double rooms and facilities include a pool and sauna. €80.

Victoria

C/Hermano Apolinar 8 ☎922 33 16 83, ⊛www.victoria.teneriffa.com. Smart but pricey lodgings in a refurbished 400-year old Canarian mansion, whose thirteen double rooms come with satellite TV, fax and modem connections. €120.

Shops

Casa de Los Turistas

C/San Francisco. Mon–Sat 9am–6pm. Free. One of the La Orotava's Doce Casas, the impressive Casa de Los Turistas is entirely devoted to pedalling Canarian handicrafts from embroidery and lace to cigars and wine. The courtyard sees occasional pottery and weaving displays and also has an example of the floor collages which decorate the town during Corpus Christi (see p.85).

Restaurants

Casa Egon

C/Leon 5 ☎922 33 00 87. Closed Sun eve and Mon. Basic, inexpensive bistro-style restaurant specializing in omelettes, tapas and classic Canarian dishes.

Victoria

Hotel Victoria ☎922 33 26 83. Tues–Sat 1–4.30pm & 8–10.30pm; Sun 1–4pm. The best place to eat in the old town centre with a lovely courtyard dining area. Expensive Canarian dishes are on the menu: the sole in prawn sauce with asparagus is especially good.

Garachico and around

Standing at the base of immense cliffs beside a deep harbour, **Garachico** was, along with La Laguna and La Orotava, one of the first towns on the island. The narrow cobbled streets, rough fishermen's cottages and grand town houses belonged to what was Tenerife's most important sixteenth-century port until a series of natural disasters – volcanic eruptions and earthquakes – plagued the town and ultimately ruined its harbour. But for visitors at least the results of these events – lava rock-pools in the town's bay and charming old streets frozen in time – are engagingly picturesque.

A good day-trip, particularly during the August Romería, the largest harvest festival-style celebration on the island, Garachico also makes a relaxing, alterna-

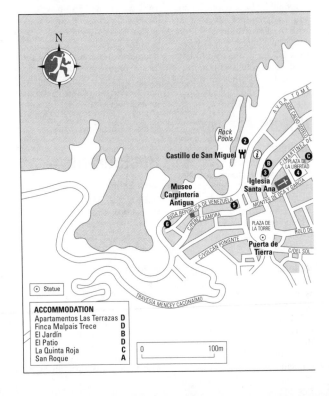

ACCOMMODATION
Apartamentos Las Terrazas **D**
Finca Malpais Trece **D**
El Jardín **B**
El Patio **D**
La Quinta Roja **C**
San Roque **A**

tive base to the big resorts and gives easy access to the neighbouring town of **Icod de los Vinos** and **El Drago**, the gigantic dragon tree there.

Arrival and information

Buses connect Garachico with other towns along the north coast, including Puerto de la Cruz (#363, 16–25 daily, 1hr) and Santa Cruz (#107, 4–6 daily, 1hr 35min). The **tourist office** is at C/Esteban Ponte 9 (Mon–Fri 10am–3pm; ☏922 83 01 85).

Castillo de San Miguel

Avda. Tome Cano. Daily 10am–6pm. €1. One of the town's oldest and most striking buildings is the stocky harbourside fort, Castillo de San Miguel. Built in the sixteenth century to protect Garachico from pirates, the small fort was one of the few buildings to survive the 1706 volcanic eruption and is now home to a vaguely diverting rock and fossil collection. More appealing are the views from the ramparts across the village and out to the Roque de Garachico, a lone rock monolith in the bay.

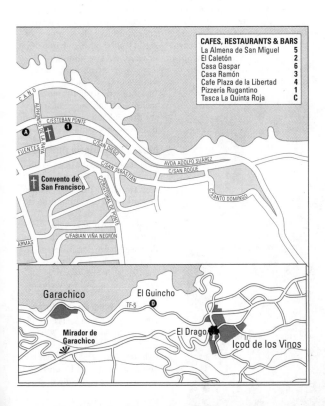

CAFES, RESTAURANTS & BARS	
La Almena de San Miguel	5
El Caletón	2
Casa Gaspar	6
Casa Ramón	3
Cafe Plaza de la Libertad	4
Pizzería Rugantino	1
Tasca La Quinta Roja	C

El Caletón rock pools

One of Garachico's unique attractions is a series of rock pools behind the Castillo de San Miguel. This area of lava is a result of the same eruption in 1706 that closed the harbour and ruined the town, but locals have made the best of it by creating paved walkways between the natural bathing pools. Formed as lava cooled on contact with the sea, these are fed and cleaned by the tidal action – making bathing possible only at low tide during calm seas.

Plaza de la Torre

Narrow Calle Esteban Ponte divides rows of elegant, largely wooden, town houses as it runs through the centre of Garachico to Plaza de Juan Gonzalez de la Torre. A small park in the square contains the **Puerta de Tierra**, a one-time gate to the town's harbour, and an old wooden winepress.

▼ NARROW ALLEY, GARACHICO

Plaza de la Libertad

The town's main square, Plaza de la Libertad, has as its centrepiece a statue of Simon Bolivar, the nineteenth-century South American freedom fighter. His tenuous connection to Garachico is through his grandmother, who emigrated from here after the 1706 disaster. On the western side of the plaza stands the grand **Iglesia Santa Ana**, the town's main church, topped by a six-storey belltower and containing a fine wooden ceiling.

Convento de San Francisco

Plaza de la Libertad. Mon–Fri 9am–7pm, Sat 9am–6pm, Sun 9am–2pm. €1. This former convent houses the small and ramshackle town museum whose collections include a number of shells, stuffed birds and an exhibit of locks and keys through the ages. More interesting is the information on Garachico's history, particularly its role as a major port, and the chance to see the building's pretty wooden balconies and atriums.

Museo Carpintería Antigua

Avda. República de Venezuela 17. Daily 9am–7pm. €1.50. Fans of the elegant woodwork on balconies around Garachico might like to visit the small Museo Carpintería Antigua. Old artisans' tools are beautifully displayed here alongside photos of their work around town, and there's also a small shop selling local products and souvenirs.

El Drago, Icod de los Vinos

Bus #106 & 108 from Santa Cruz, 15 daily, 1hr 10min–1hr 35min; #354 & #363 from Puerto de la Cruz, 32–41 daily, 1hr 10min; #363 from Garachico, 16–25 daily, 15min. El Drago, the world's oldest and biggest

The Dragon Tree

Once common around the Mediterranean, successive ice ages pushed the **dragon tree** (*dracaena draco*) further south around twenty million years ago, restricting its habitat to the climatically stable Canary Islands.

The tree's unusual characteristics – gnarled wood and geometric buds – and its longevity earned it much reverence in the past. Guanche elders and kings held court beneath their canopies and believed the tree foretold the future – a fine blossom pointing to a fine harvest. The dragon tree's most striking feature, the red rubbery sap, or dragon's blood, not only gave the tree its name but has also been put to a variety of uses. The Guanches incorporated it into healing salves and even in their mummification process, while more recently it has been used to dye toothpaste, marble and Italian violins. High demand for the sap meant, however, that many dragon trees were tapped to death, and today there are few large specimens left on the island.

specimen of the endemic giant yucca-like dragon tree, towers above the main road on the western side of Icod de los Vinos. Its dimensions are impressive enough – seventeen metres high with a six metre trunk circumference – but its true claim to fame arises from its age, thought to be at least 500 years – which means it pre-dates even the oldest buildings that surround it.

The tree stands in a garden, to which admission is charged (€3), but most visitors are content to view it from an adjacent elevated shady square where the Baroque interior of the late sixteenth-century **Iglesia de San Marcos** is also worth a look.

▼ EL DRAGO

Hotels

Finca Malpais Trece

El Guincho ☎ & ☏922 13 30 68.
Large old farmhouse on the
same estate as the *Hotel El Patio*
(see below) which has incredible
views across plantations to the
coast from its courtyard and
sun-terrace. Bathing is possible
in a rocky bay, a ten minute
walk through the banana groves.
€48.

El Patio

El Guincho ☎922 13 32 80,
☺www.hotelpatio.com.
Inconspicuously signposted from
the road to Icod de los Vinos at
El Guincho, this sixteenth-
century hotel is tucked away in
the middle of a massive banana
plantation. Its airy rooms are set
around a grand and impressively
lush courtyard, and facilities
include a swimming pool. Rates
include breakfast. €90.

La Quinta Roja

Plaza de la Libertad ☎922 13 33 77,
☺www.quintaroja.com. Recently
opened hotel in a refurbished
sixteenth-century building
noted for its wonderful
woodwork and airy courtyard.
Rooms are simple, with
minimalist furnishings
complementing traditional
design. €120.

San Roque

C/Esteban Ponte 32 ☎922 13 34 35,
☺www.hotelsanroque.com. Once the
home of the town's leading
family, this atmospheric old
town house is now an elegant
hotel. No two rooms are the
same, but all are equipped with
TV, video and minibar, and
there's also a gourmet
restaurant, rooftop-terrace and
pool. Some singles available and
all rates include breakfast. €150.

Pensions

El Jardín

C/Esteban de Ponte 8 ☎922 83 02 45,
☺argonaut@arrakis.es. Impressively
creaky and atmospheric old
town house set around a
sociable central courtyard with
its own little bar. Rooms are
large and simple, and most share
bathrooms. The owners speak
English and also let a couple of
apartments. Rooms €24;
apartments €36.

Apartments

Apartamentos Las Terrazas

El Guincho ☎ & ☏922 13 31 20 or 619
13 31 20. A small, modern block
of self-catering apartments
tucked away in a peaceful
banana plantation (see *Hotel El
Patio* above). The roomy units
are simply and stylishly
furnished, and have private
balconies with views towards
the coast. Weekly rates available.
€36–48.

Cafés

El Caletón

Avda. Tome Cano, Garachico.
Wonderfully located between
the Castillo de San Miguel and
the rock pools, this cafe is the
ideal place for a drink and light
snack while you enjoy the view.
There's also a more substantial
selection of reasonably priced
fish and meat dishes.

Cafe Plaza de la Libertad

Plaza de la Libertad, Garachico. Kiosk
surrounded by outdoor seating
in the town's leafy central
square, where families and
friends gather to sit and socialize
at any time of day.

Restaurants

La Almena de San Miguel

Avda. República de Venezuela 4,
Garachico. Unprepossessing first-
floor restaurant that's
nevertheless an excellent choice
for fresh seafood at low prices –
as the regular presence of locals
suggests.

Casa Gaspar

Avda. República de Venezuela 20,
Garachico. Closed Sun. More
expensive and grander than
most of the town's restaurants,
this place is a safe bet for good
seafood. There's always a
selection of the local catch on
display, priced by weight.

Casa Ramón

C/Esteban de Ponte 4, Garachico. Basic
restaurant that's recommended
not so much for the limited
menu of excellent seafood dishes,
or the distinctive, spicy home-
made *mojo*, but more for its old,
dingy wood-clad atmosphere and
its elderly proprietor, who makes
you feel as though you've
dropped by your Canarian
grandmother's for lunch.

Pizzería Rugantino

C/Esteban de Ponte 44, Garachico. Fri,
Sat & Sun 7pm–midnight. Small and
invariably packed restaurant that
serves arguably the best pizzas in
Tenerife – bargains at around
€6. You may to have to wait for
a table but it's worth it.

Bars

Tasca La Quinta Roja

Plaza de la Libertad. Open late.
Traditional wood-and-tile tasca
– at the back of the hotel *La
Quinta Roja* – which, in the
absence of any real nightlife in
Garachico, is the best place to
go for an evening drink.

▼ CAFE PLAZA DE LA LIBERTAD

The Teno

The colossal and ancient **Teno Mountains** define Tenerife's northwest tip. They're an excellent area for **hiking**, with steep gorges and ravines carved out of volcanic rock and cutting down to the rugged coastline and a few accessible beaches. Unlike the laurel forests

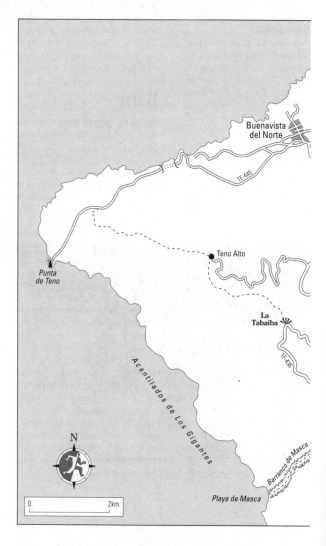

of the Anaga region, the landscape here is largely tree-less – most of its timber was cleared to fire sugar mills in the sixteenth century – but this allows clearer views of local peaks like **Montaña Jala**. The premier attraction, however, is the remote village of **Masca**, deep in the middle of the range, from where the region's best-known hike follows the **Barranco de Masca** gorge to the sea.

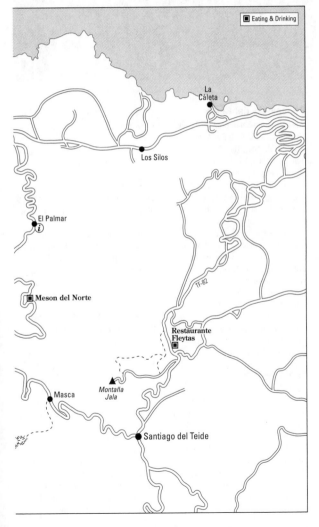

▲ LOS GIGANTES CLIFFS FROM PUNTA DE TENO

Buenavista del Norte

Bus #107 from Santa Cruz, 4–6 daily,
1hr 35min; #363 from Puerto de la
Cruz, 16–25 daily, 1hr 15min; and #363
from Garachico, 16–25 daily, 15min.
Buenavista del Norte is the
largest of several uneventful
towns squeezed onto the
northern coast beside the sheer
sides of the Teno massif. As
terminus for local and island-
wide bus services, it's a useful
transport hub and the small
collection of seafood restaurants
is a boon for weary hikers. A
large golf course being
completed on the edge of
Buenavista looks likely to change
the focus for this town that has
until now relied on banana
cultivation for its income.

Punta de Teno

The Punta de Teno, a jagged
volcanic-rock headland jutting
into the ocean, is Tenerife's most
westerly point. Marked by an old
lighthouse, fishing off the
headland attracts local fishermen
and the clear waters of its
sheltered bay invite bathing, but
it's the views from the rocky
promontory itself that most come
for, particularly at sunset when

the last rays disappear behind La
Gomera and La Palma. Equally
impressive are the views eastwards
towards the Teno mountains and
the huge coastal cliffs.

El Palmar

Bus #355 or #366 from Buenavista, 16
daily, 10min. Among a handful of
small rural settlements in the
heart of the Teno, the main
reason to stop in El Palmar is to
visit the **park information
centre** (Mon–Fri 8am–3pm),
which hands out free, but fairly
simple, hiking maps.

Mirador La Tabaiba & hike

Bus #355 from Buenavista, 4 daily,
20min. The best views over the
northern Teno are from Mirador
La Tabaiba at its southern edge,
with the most spectacular being
north towards Buenavista or west
over uninhabited gorges and
massive cliffs to the ocean. The
viewpoint also marks the start of
an excellent ridge walk back to
Buenavista, some 11km away.
The four-hour hike begins by
heading past grazing goats and,
in spring, wildflower meadows,
to the village of Teno Alto. From
here, continue through the

village on the minor road that soon becomes a track and gently climbs before finally descending steeply to the road between Buenavista and Punta de Teno. From here you can turn left for an easy 4km return walk to Punta de Teno or right to head 6km along the lightly used road back to Buenavista, with views of the mountains and coast for company.

Montaña Jala hike

Bus #325 from Puerto de la Cruz, 6 daily, 1hr 15min; or Los Gigantes, 6 daily, 30min. The hike up Montaña Jala at the western perimeter of the Teno range is one of the easier walks in this area, climbing through a mix of vegetation – including some prime laurel forest – and rewarded with some great views. The best place to start the hike is the roadside **Restaurant Fleytas** – buses between Icod de Los Viños and Las Américas stop here and private vehicles can be left in the car park – from where the eight-kilometre loop up Montaña Jala takes around three hours.

The **trail** begins opposite the restaurant, immediately descending into a wide valley where it passes some ponds and then zigzags up to a ridge on the right, where it splits into three. Take the narrow track straight ahead through thick vegetation; the trail here is overgrown and in places difficult to follow. Look out for a fairly well-trodden path branching off on the uphill side and follow it to a wider track, where you turn right, following it a short way, before climbing again on a small track. This short path soon follows a stream-bed before it leads out to a forestry road that circles Montaña Jala. To climb to the summit turn left here; around half an hour later you'll be rewarded with phenomenal views from the summit. The hiking loop ends by descending down the summit road, turning left off it just shy of the main road, then descending on the narrow track that leads back to the ponds and restaurant.

Masca

Bus #355 from Buenavista, 4 daily, 25min; or Valle Santiago, 4 daily, 30min. The village of Masca, in an isolated and picturesque gorge, is considered Tenerife's

▼ THE ROAD TO MASCA

prettiest village, and, outside the hours of 11am–5pm, when crowds and tour buses take over, it's hard to disagree. The village was only connected to the outside world in 1991 by a steep winding road that brings visitors in to see its old stone houses looking out across palm trees and improbably steep ravines towards the Atlantic. The fertile soil here once supported a population of six hundred, but this has dropped to around one hundred today, and many of the buildings have been converted into restaurants or gift shops, with most villagers remaining only to service tourists.

Barranco de Masca hike

One of the best hikes on the island is the strenuous, six-hour return trek down the steep-sided Barranco de Masca. Beginning in Masca village, the route ends at a small beach surrounded by the staggering Acantilados de Los Gigantes (see opposite) and is a must for any relatively experienced hiker. The path starts just left of the ridge that runs through the centre of town. Keep an eye out for markers along the way as you pass through ravines as high as 600m above the sea. At its narrowest – and most memorable – the gorge is only twenty-metres wide, and filled with bizarre, swirling rock formations and curious vegetation.

Several companies (see p.171) offer **hiking trips** down the valley from the main coastal resorts, costing €35–45 and usually offering a shuttle bus to Masca and a **boat** to pick you up from the beach at the end. If you want to organize your own transport to the village, but would like to take a boat from the beach to Los Gigantes,

contact Excursions Marítimas (☎922 86 19 18) who charge €9 for this service; the boat leaves the beach at 3.30pm.

Accommodation

El Guanche

Masca ☎922 86 14 05. Basic rooms (with outside toilet) in Masca's old schoolhouse. As the only accommodation in the village it's the best chance to see it without the droves of day-trippers. Rates include half-board. €48–60.

Restaurants

La Fuente

Masca. Daily noon–6pm. Superbly positioned below the main road near the village church, this place has great views over the valley from its terrace and is consequently one of Masca's busiest restaurants. Serves excellent home-made lemonade as well as good Canarian food.

Meson del Norte

Carretera de Masca. Closed Mon. Large rural restaurant, 6km south of Buenavista on the road to Masca, offering inexpensive but top-quality upland Canarian fare – mostly grilled meat and chicken – along with fresh goat's cheese and local wines that are well worth sampling. Other restaurants further up the road to Masca are similar.

El Pescador

C/Los Molinos 27, Buenavista del Norte. Wed–Mon 9am–midnight. In the centre of Buenavista, "The fisherman" has a great range of inexpensive seafood, including succulent king prawns in three different sauces.

The west coast

Though large-scale resort developments are beginning to creep up Tenerife's **west coast**, the main resorts here – **Los Gigantes**, **Puerto de Santiago** and **Playa de la Arena** – offer a low-key alternative to Playa de Las Américas to the south, and attract those looking for good weather and a quiet resort; nightlife is almost entirely absent here. All three lie at the northern end of this stretch of coast, huddled beside the colossal **Acantilados de Los Gigantes** (Giants' Cliffs), while the small towns further south mostly exist to service the resorts but at least have a Canarian feel to them. **Alcalá** is set on a pretty bay and **Playa San Juan** recently invested in a beach and attractive coastal promenade. Inland, this region is thick with (mainly banana) plantations between a series of forgettable towns: only **Adeje**, at the southern end above Las Américas, is worth a visit, particularly to hike up the **Barranco del Infierno**.

Los Gigantes town

Though largely characterized by densely packed low-rise apartment complexes, the town of Los Gigantes has the advantage of a spectacular setting beside the huge cliffs from which it gets its name. A single, one-way main road descends into town and loops around its central collection of shops, which hide a tiny pedestrian plaza in their centre. Below this commercial area is a pleasant marina, crowded with boats and lined with cafés and restaurants, and a black sandy beach, accessed by an alley behind the marina.

▼ LOS GIGANTES MARINA

Acantilados de los Gigantes

Beyond the beach on the northern edge of Los Gigantes town rise the sheer rock walls of the massive Acantilados de Los Gigantes (Giants' Cliffs). Formed by lava being squeezed under high pressure through multiple parallel cracks, these astounding formations rise 500m out of the sea. A popular day-trip destination. most visitors explore them on boat tours, which also head out to the Gomeran Channel to see dolphins and stop for a swim.

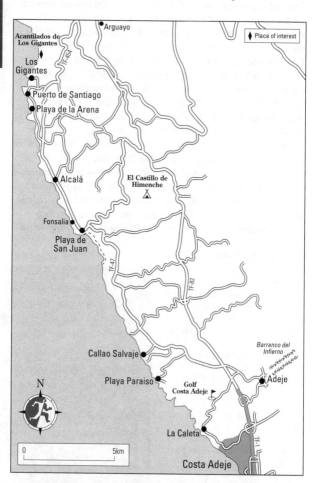

Arrival and information

Buses connect **Los Gigantes**, **Puerto de Santiago** and **Playa de la Arena** – all just a couple of minutes from each other – with the island-wide network: bus #325 from Puerto de la Cruz (6 daily, 1hr 45min); #473 from Las Galletas (15 daily, 1hr 40min) via Los Cristianos and Las Américas. The local **tourist office** overlooks the beach in Playa de la Arena at Edificio Seguro de Sol 36–37 (Mon–Fri 9.30am–3.30pm, Sat 9.30am–12.30pm; ☎922 86 03 48),.

▲ PLAYA DE LA ARENA

Expect to pay from around €18 per person for these trips, which are hawked by a number of operators based beside the town's marina.

Los Gigantes Lidos

The opportunity to swim along the coast beside Los Gigantes is often compromised by huge waves and dangerous undercurrents. To compensate, two private complexes offer pools and sun terraces on cliffs above the sea, just south of the marina in Los Gigantes. The larger of the two, El Laguillo (daily 10.30am–6.30pm; €4, kids €2) has a more imaginatively laid-out bathing area, with lakes, waterfalls and islands, than the nearby Oasis (daily 10am–6pm; €3, kids €1.50), which is duller but greener.

Puerto de Santiago and Playa de la Arena

Merging with Los Gigantes and each other, Puerto de Santiago and Playa de la Arena hold an unexciting mixture of modern, sprawling homes, hotels and apartments with most restaurants, bars and cafés situated along the main seafront road. The local highlight is the small and busy black-sand beach from which Playa de la Arena gets its name.

Alcalá and Playa de San Juan

Bus #473 from Las Galletas via Los Cristianos and Las Américas, 15 daily, 1hr 30min; and Los Gigantes, 15 daily, 10–20min. Set amid banana plantations, the unpretentious town of Alcalá centres on a plaza near the small sheltered harbour and beach which is good for a quiet swim. Further south along the main road, Playa de San Juan is recommended for its large and uncrowded pebble beach and long coastal promenade which snakes its way from the town onto adjoining cliffs for a pleasant two-kilometre hike with excellent views over the ocean.

▼ PLAYA DE SAN JUAN

Adeje

Bus #416 or #473 from Las Américas and Los Cristianos, 36 daily, 30min; bus #473 from Los Gigantes, 15 daily, 40min and Las Galletas, 60min. Though much of the administrative town of Adeje is bland, its location and modern centre are pretty enough. The only sights are the fortified hacienda, **Casa Fuerte** – sacked by Sir Francis Drake in 1586 and not open to visitors – and the simply decorated sixteenth-century **Iglesia de Santa Ursula** at the top of the main road, Calle Grande. The church's white-washed walls and *Mudéjar* wooden roof protect a copy of the famous Virgin of Candelaria (see p.71).

▲ BARRANCO DEL INFIERNO WATERFALL

Barranco del Infierno hike

6km/4hr return hike. Close to Adeje – and the main reason for coming here – is the **Barranco del Infierno** (Hell's Ravine), the deepest gorge in the Canaries and location of Tenerife's only year-round stream. The path, beginning uphill of the Casa Fuerte in Adeje and beside the panoramic terrace of the restaurant *Otello*, is easy to follow and involves little steep climbing. The route offers dizzying views down the ravine and passes through a varied landscape where semi-desert gives way to thick stands of willow and eucalyptus trees before finishing at a rather disappointing waterfall which does, however, afford the chance of a cold dip.

Hotels

Barceló Santiago

C/La Hondura 8, Puerto Santiago ☎922 86 09 12, ⊛www.barcelo.com. Cliff-top hotel centred on a massive sun deck and pool. Facilities include a fitness centre and tennis and squash courts, while most rooms have a balcony overlooking the sea with views of La Gomera. €132.

Fonda Central

C/Grande 26, Adeje ☎922 78 15 50. Beautifully restored eighteenth-century Canarian family residence on Adeje's main street. All rooms are on the top floor and look onto a central courtyard. Rates include breakfast. €90.

Playa La Arena

C/Lajial 4, Playa de la Arena ☎922 79 57 78, ⊕www.springhoteles.com. Large hotel containing over four hundred air-conditioned rooms, most with balcony and sea views. Facilities include three bars, a restaurant (with a good breakfast buffet), two large pools (featuring waterfalls and a waterslide), tennis courts and a minigolf course. €132.

Pensions

Alcalá

C/Marruecos 2, Alcalá ☎922 86 54 57. Bohemian place just north of the harbour, run by an eccentric Gomeran who provides leaflets on his life as a South American revolutionary. The influences of his adventures are evidenced by his abstract paintings on the guesthouse walls, while the rooms, though less interesting, are clean and modern. €25.

Rambala

C/Grande 7, Adeje ☎922 78 00 71. Plain rooms, with bathroom and balcony, on the town's main street. €24.

Pensión Rochil

C/Corpus Christi 29, Adeje ☎922 78 02 52. Scrupulously clean lodgings on a minor road running parallel to the town's main thoroughfare. Good long-stay rates can be negotiated. €22.

Apartments

Aparthotel Poblado Marinero

C/Poblado Marinero, Los Gigantes ☎922 86 09 66, ⊕pobladomarinero @cajacanarias.net. Attractive Canarian-village-style complex beside Los Gigantes port and with its own rock-pool swimming area. Apartments have a kitchen, bathroom and lounge and can sleep up to six. €48.

Apartamentos Neptuno-Cristina

Avda. Maritima 24, Playa de la Arena ☎922 86 16 06, ⊕922 86 05 84. Large, well-equipped apartments in a modest complex containing a small pool and sun deck next to the black sands of Playa de la Arena. The friendly local owners offer one- and two-bed apartments for weekly rental, sleeping two to four people, and there are a number of shops and restaurants close to the complex. €45.

Shops

Blanca

C/Grande 59, Adeje. Mon–Fri 9am–1pm & 4.30–8pm, Sat 9am–1.30pm. In business for over 50 years, this shop on Adeje's main street is a good place to browse through a medley of antiques and knick-knacks, from furniture and old phones to sewing machines.

Centro Alfarero

Arguayo ☎922 86 31 27. Tues–Sat 10am–1pm & 4–7pm, Sun 10am–2pm. For the chance to watch rough-hewn traditional pots being made using thousand-year-old Guanche techniques, this is the place to come. There's also a small shop selling the finished goods.

Restaurants

La Barrera

C/Los Tarajales, Fonsalia. Closed Sun. Local tapas bar and restaurant in a tiny village midway between Alcalá and San Juan. The TV might be blaring but the food is inexpensive and first-class.

Beeches

CC Santiago II, Puerto de Santiago
☎922 86 24 03. Open for dinner only,
closed Fri. Small restaurant beside
the *Hotel Barceló Santiago*
offering plenty of fresh gourmet
options, including quite a few
veggie choices. Prices border on
expensive but the food is
prepared with considerable
attention to detail. Reservations
advisable.

Casa Pancho

Avda. Marítima, Playa de la Arena
☎922 86 13 23. Closed Mon & June.
Pleasant, moderately expensive
Canarian restaurant in a great
location directly beside the
beach. Among the great fish
dishes is a delicious two-person
paella.

Restaurante Marinero

C/Los Gios Playa, Los Gigantes ☎922
86 19 55. Beautifully situated
beside the Acantilados de los
Gigantes and accessed via the
pedestrian road behind the
marina, this friendly restaurant is
the highlight of the Los
Gigantes dining scene. It
specializes in moderately priced
fresh fish and sea food –
recommended is the fish soup,
oven-baked platters and, for
dessert, the banana flambé.

Miranda

C/Flor de Pascua 25, Los Gigantes
☎922 86 02 07. Good and
unusually imaginative Canarian
restaurant in the centre of Los
Gigantes, where local specialities
are blended with international
cuisine to produce interesting
results at above average prices.
Vegetarians will find a couple of
(odd) choices here too.

Oasis

C/Grande 5, Adeje. Closed Wed. Adeje
has a reputation for good
upland Canarian food,
particularly garlic chicken, and
this is the only dish available at
Oasis, served with salad and fries
at crowded tables on the tree-
lined main road.

Otelo

C/Los Molinos, Adeje ☎922 78 03 74.
Wed–Mon 11am–10.30pm. The
unbeatable views over the
Barranco del Infierno from its
patio make this touristy
restaurant the pick of the bunch.
The garlic chicken is excellent
and prices are very reasonable.

El Pescador de Alcalá

Muelle, Alcalá. Big place with
moderate prices and harbour
views that's an excellent option
for fresh fish, straight from the
restaurant's tanks.

Los Cristianos, Las Américas and Costa Adeje

The three-kilometre-long string of hotel and apartment complexes along Tenerife's southwest coast may divide into different districts – **Los Cristianos, Playa de Las Américas, Costa Adeje** – but in reality it's one single conurbation, accommodating two-thirds of the island's visitors and countless expatriates. The districts have characters that range from down-at-heel to fairly exclusive, but, with the exception of the core of the old harbour town of Los Cristianos, all of them have been built from scratch in the last thirty years. Water was piped in and sand imported to make beaches, and while the scale of this achievement is undoubtedly impressive, if you're looking for a holiday to get away from it all and enjoy some of the island's indigenous charm, you'll be disappointed. Most visitors spend the bulk of their time on crowded beaches, though water sports, including some decent surfing and diving, are also possible and several commercial parks and attractions are within easy reach, most providing free transport. This mega tourist city also has the benefit of good infrastructure, which makes it easy to escape to Tenerife's quieter parts by bus or rental car.

Arrival and information

Most package holidays include a transfer to your hotel, but there's also a frequent **public bus** from the airport which passes through Los Cristianos and southern Las Américas before heading for the **bus station**, between central Las Américas, San Eugenio and the motorway.

Las Américas has two **tourist offices**. The centre and north is covered by the Adeje-region office at Avda. Rafael Puig 1 (Mon–Fri 9am–1pm; ☎922 75 06 33), just north of CC Veronicas in central Las Américas, while the south is covered by the Arona region office near the Parque Santiago II building (Mon–Fri 9am–1pm & 4–7pm, Sat 9am–1pm; ☎922 79 76 68, ☻www.arona.org). The tourist office in Los Cristianos (Mon–Fri 9am–3.30pm, Sat 9am–1pm) is downhill from the bus station in the town's cultural centre.

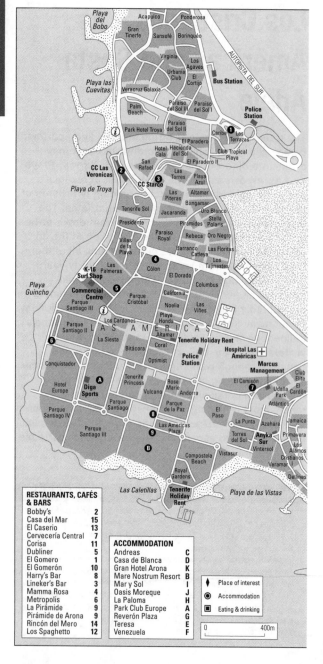

RESTAURANTS, CAFÉS & BARS

Bobby's	2
Casa del Mar	15
El Caserio	13
Cervecería Central	7
Corisa	11
Dubliner	5
El Gomero	1
El Gomerón	10
Harry's Bar	8
Lineker's Bar	3
Mamma Rosa	4
Metropolis	6
La Pirámide	9
Pirámide de Arona	9
Rincón del Mero	14
Los Spaghetto	12

ACCOMMODATION

Andreas	C
Casa de Blanca	D
Gran Hotel Arona	K
Mare Nostrum Resort	B
Mar y Sol	I
Oasis Moreque	J
La Paloma	H
Park Club Europe	A
Reverón Plaza	G
Teresa	E
Venezuela	F

♦ Place of interest
◉ Accommodation
■ Eating & drinking

0 _____ 400m

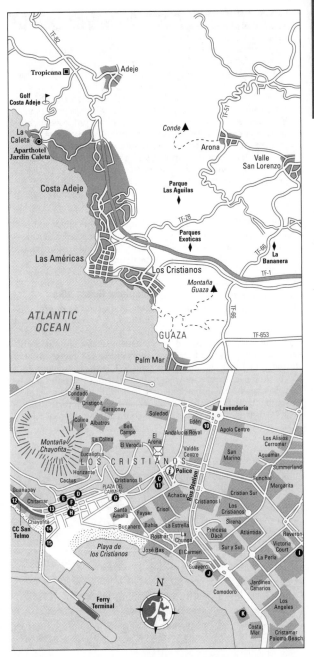

Whale and dolphin watching

Whale and dolphin watching trips are a popular excursion from the resorts and companies offering them can be found in harbourside booths in Los Cristianos and in Las Américas at Puerto Colón. As many as twenty-six species of whale and dolphin have been spotted in the channel between Tenerife and La Gomera, though you're most likely to see pilot whales and bottlenose, striped or Atlantic spotted dolphins. Two- to three-hour trips (around €12 per person) head out to the whales and dolphins and stop for a swim and a picnic on the boat. Longer trips – typically five hours for around €30 per person – will also cruise to the imposing cliffs of Los Gigantes (see p.101). The boats used range from old wooden vessels to luxury yachts, but the most important thing to check when booking is whether the trip is actually to do some whale-spotting or if it's just a so-called "booze cruise". Some operators also offer deep-sea fishing trips, starting from around €48 per person for a five-hour trip.

Los Cristianos

Nestling beside Montaña Chayofita, adjacent to its beach and harbour, the old pedestrian core of Los Cristianos is easy to identify and worth a visit. Having grown from fishing village to port and then, since the 1960s, into an agreeable resort, it's still home to many Canarians. Away from the old centre, however, it's a different story, and high-rise apartment blocks dominate here as much as they do elsewhere. A promenade passes the harbour and the Playa de los Cristianos on its route along the town's entire seafront before joining the promenade that runs around Las Américas by the new and relatively uncrowded Playa de las Vistas.

Montaña Guaza hike

3km/3hr. To the east of Los Cristianos, the promenade heads past high-rise hotel blocks and restaurants before finishing just short of the 428-metre Montaña Guaza. The shadeless climb to the peak from this point follows a clear route that crosses arid terrain via a steep rocky path before reaching terraced farm

▼ LOS CRISTIANOS HARBOUR

▲ SURFERS AT LAS AMÉRICAS

land higher up. The reward for your troubles is a view from the summit that stretches over Los Cristianos, Las Américas and the ocean as far as La Gomera.

Southern Las Américas

Projecting a relatively exclusive image and with some of the least crowded beaches, southern Las Américas is easily one of the most attractive districts along this stretch of coast. Its pride is the five-star **Mare Nostrum Resort**, whose extravagant 1980s architecture – an oversized pastiche of Mexico's Chichén Itzá pyramids – makes it an eye-catching landmark. Far more natural is the Playa de Guincho, beside one of the prettiest stretches of Las Américas' promenade. This narrow and rocky beach, popular with local surfers and bodyboarders, is one of the few natural stretches of coastline on this part of the island.

Northern Las Américas

Northern Las Américas is almost solely responsible for Las Américas' notoriety as a concrete jungle of tackiness and hedonism. Thrown up in the 1970s to cash in on the booming tourist trade, by the mid-1980s it had become tatty and unappealing and has largely remained so, despite attempts at improvement. The bland concrete commercial centres at the heart of the resort – CC Veronicas and CC Starco –

house the throbbing nightlife for which the resort is notorious and which forms the main attraction for many young visitors to the island. By day there's not much going on in the bars and fast-food outlets here, but by night the area is packed with clubbers.

Aquapark Octopus

San Eugenio ☎922 71 52 66. Daily 10am–6pm. €14, under-14s €9. Free buses from marked stops along the seafront road in Las Américas and near the bus station in Los Cristianos. Along with the usual array of pools, slides and waterfalls, this water park also puts on two daily dolphin shows (Mon–Fri 1pm & 3pm, Sat & Sun 3pm). The complex is best visited on Tuesdays or Fridays – the main flight days when many holiday-makers are busy travelling – and

▼ AQUAPARK OCTOPUS

avoided at weekends, when local kids often take over. The park has several cafés and bars but they're quite pricey so packing a lunch is a good idea.

Costa Adeje

Though in practical terms a continuation of Las Américas, its location in a different administrative district means that the area of resort development north of Las Veronicas is known as the Costa Adeje.

At its southern end lie the overwhelmingly British-dominated adjacent districts of Torviscas and San Eugenio; both successful if dull family destinations where you'll find the small marina of Puerto Colón. The beaches are similarly very popular but generally crowded. Set in a small bay and beside Puerto Colón, Playa de Torviscas is marginally the most attractive option, with kayaks, pedalos, jet skis and inflatable bananas all available for hire.

▲ FAÑABÉ

North of San Eugenio is the newer and considerably smarter resort of **Fañabé**. At the northern end of this district the *Gran Hotel Melia Bahía del Duque* is the island's most luxurious accommodation and the area's most significant landmark. Smartly dressed visitors (no shorts) are welcome to wander around the complex from 6.30pm onwards – worthwhile since several buildings in the complex are reproductions of notable buildings around the island. The Playa de Fañabé beach is relatively quiet and the pick of the bunch along the Costa Adeje.

La Caleta and Golf Costa Adeje

Bus #441 from Los Cristianos via Las Américas, 11 daily, 35min. Las Américas' string of hotels comes to an end just short of the relatively peaceful fishing village of La Caleta, noted for its fresh fish restaurants and rocky bay offering decent snorkelling. Inland a grid of roads have been

▼ GOLF COSTA ADEJE

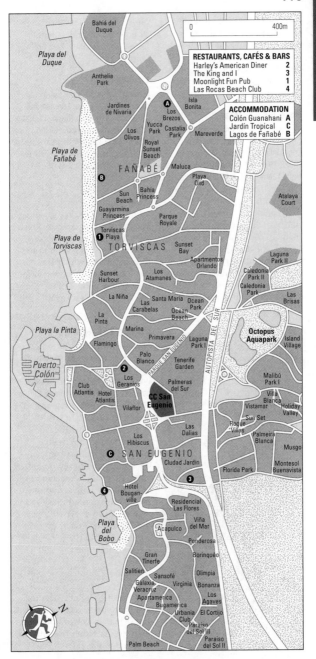

RESTAURANTS, CAFÉS & BARS

Harley's American Diner 2
The King and I 3
Moonlight Fun Pub 1
Las Rocas Beach Club 4

ACCOMMODATION

Colón Guanahani A
Jardín Tropical C
Lagos de Fañabé B

laid out to accommodate new developments but for now a stretch of wasteland separates La Caleta and the rest of Las Américas from the large and exclusive golf course, Costa Adeje (see p.112).

Parques Exóticas

TF-66 road, parallel to Autopista del Sur, exit 26. Five free buses daily from Los Cristianos and Las Américas, call ☎922 79 54 24 for locations and times. Daily 10am–6pm. €10, under-13s €6. This well designed zoo and park is a big hit with kids – and photographers – thanks to its policy of allowing visitors into many of the animal enclosures. One highlight, Amazonia, is a huge tent full of rainforest flora and fauna – including a selection of exotic birds – and while Cactus Park is perhaps only for

▾ PARQUE LAS ÁGUILAS

die-hard cactus fans, the bat cave, butterfly garden, reptile house and monkey area are all worth a visit.

La Bananera

Buzanada. Autopista del Sur exit 26, direction Valle de San Lorenzo ☎922 72 04 03. Daily tours 10am, 11.30am, 1pm, 3.30pm & 4.15pm. €7.50, under-13s €3, under-4s free. The region's most refreshingly low-key attraction is La Bananera, an adapted family farm giving tours on Tenerife's agriculture with emphasis – as the name would suggest – on explaining banana cultivation. Tours finish with a look at a number of endemic species grown in the farm's gardens, which also produce some of the ingredients used in the good-value set meals offered in the **restaurant** (daily noon–4pm).

Parque Las Águilas

Chayofa. Autopista del Sur exit 27, direction Arona. Free shuttle buses from Las Américas, Los Cristianos, Puerto de la Cruz and Los Gigantes, call ☎922 72 90 10 for times and pick-up points. Daily 10am–6pm. €17, under-13s €8. Parque Las Águilas is one of southern Tenerife's premier attractions, with a sizeable collection of animal enclosures chaotically organized amongst the lush vegetation of its replicated jungle. The main attractions are the bird shows, especially the displays of birds of prey who swoop low over the crowds – sit on the lower rows for maximum effect – and there's also an assault course with a bobsleigh run (€2.50 per run) that's popular with kids. Be aware that on windy days the shows are likely to be cancelled, and bring a picnic if you want to avoid the rather over-priced restaurants and cafés.

▲ ROQUE DEL CONDE

Arona and Conde hike

Bus #480 or #482 from Los Cristianos, 16 daily, 20min. Arona's tiny centre is good for a stroll and for a quick look at the seventeenth-century Iglesia San Antonio Abad. The town is also the starting point for the hike up the thousand-metre-high flat-topped Conde (4hr return) from where there are rewarding views over southern Tenerife and La Gomera. Most of the shadeless route follows a steep path along an old pack-road though the irregularly spaced painted waymarks occasionally deviate from this. To find the trailhead, leave the plaza in front of the church by the road that runs uphill to the left and cross the main road onto an unmarked road. After a couple of bends this road straightens, leaving town in the direction of the mountain. Turn left at a statue of Jesus and right at C/Vento 30. From here, painted trail markers follow a route that immediately crosses a gorge and then heads up the left-hand side of the hill, the path getting steeper and steeper until it reaches the summit.

Hotels

Andreas

C/Antigua General Franco, Los Cristianos ☎922 79 00 24, ⊛www.hotelesreveron.com. Functional hotel, close to the centre of town. Many of the ample rooms have balconies, some of which face a busy road, and all have private bathroom. €50.

Colón Guanahani

C/Bruselas, Playa de Fañabé, Costa Adeje ☎922 71 23 14, ⓔnivaria@nexo.es. Massive and stylish four-star hotel whose 1500 rooms are plush, spacious and have generous balconies. Facilities include a sauna and pool, and guests are offered reduced fees at local golf courses. Substantial reductions for stays of five nights or more. €94.

Gran Hotel Arona

Avda Marítima, Los Cristianos ☎922 75 06 78, ⓕ922 75 02 43. Large classy hotel beside the promenade. All rooms have balconies with sea views as well as satellite TV and a minibar, and there's also an extensive sun terrace and pools. €130.

Gran Hotel Melia Bahía del Duque

Fañabé ☎922 71 30 00, ⊕www.bahia-duque.com. Luxurious modern development – in an area largely devoid of amenities – with extensive facilities including eight restaurants, nine bars, an Internet café, a library, an observatory, five swimming pools, squash and tennis courts and a jogging path. One particularly well-appointed building, the *Casas Ducales*, even has its own butler service. If money is no object, ask for the royal suite at around €1200 per night. €354.

Jardín Tropical

San Eugenio, Costa Adeje ☎922 74 60 00, ⊕www.tropical-hoteles.com. Moorish-style hotel with a sense of taste that's lacking in the surrounding architecture. Its central courtyards are filled with subtropical gardens and facilities include a large fitness centre and five good restaurants, open to non-guests, who can also use the pools for €3 per day in the adjoining Las Rocas Beach Club. Low season deals can cut prices by fifty percent. €130.

Mare Nostrum Resort

Avda. Las Américas, Las Américas ☎922 75 75 45, ⊕www.expogrupo .com. Incorporating five five-star hotels – the *Mediterranean Palace*, *Sir Anthony*, *Julio Cesar*, *Marco Antonio* and *Cleopatra Palace* – this huge complex offers a vast range of facilities including twelve restaurants and cafés, several pools, a volleyball and football area, a nudist zone, tennis and squash courts and a top-notch spa. The location – in the thick

of things near Los Cristianos – and the genuinely friendly staff are unbeatable. €110.

Oasis Moreque

Avda. Penetración, Los Cristianos ☎922 79 03 66, ⊕www.h10.es. Late Sixties building with fairly swish rooms and good facilities including a pool and tennis courts. Independent reservations are only accepted a couple of days in advance. Rates are generally reasonable – particularly the half-price single rooms – and include a good breakfast. €118.

Park Club Europe

Avda. Rafael Puig, Las Américas ☎922 75 70 60, ⊕pce@europe-hotels.org. Comfortable hotel with good sports facilities, as well as a scuba-diving outfit and the hiking- and mountain-biking tour operator, Diga Sports (see p.171). The reasonably sized rooms boast understated decor and large balconies, and rates halve in low season. €60.

Reverón Plaza

Plaza del Carmen, Los Cristianos ☎922 75 71 20, ⊕www.hotelesreveron.com. Swanky modern hotel whose amenities include a pool on the roof. There are great views, particularly from the exclusive *Mirador Plaza* restaurant, while the spacious rooms are tastefully decorated and have balconies. Good single rates. €100.

Pensions

Casa de Blanca

C/Ramón Pino 28, Los Cristianos ☎922 75 19 75. Situated in a quiet side-street, this basic, clean pension has rudimentary rooms with shared bathrooms. No singles, but one good-value triple. €25.

La Paloma

C/Paloma 7, Los Cristianos ☎922 79 01 98. Pleasant, if basic, rooms, most sharing bathrooms, in the pedestrianized centre of Los Cristianos. Several singles available. €25.

Teresa

C/Ramón Pino 44, Los Cristianos ☎922 79 12 30. Newly renovated, friendly boarding house on a quiet side street. The basic rooms all have shared baths. Singles available. €25.

Venezuela

Avda. de Suecia 24B, Los Cristianos ☎922 79 79 31. Located on a busy and noisy road but with clean, spartan rooms (shared bathrooms), this place offers the best deals in town for lone travellers. €23.

Apartments

Aparthotel Jardin Caleta

La Caleta ☎922 71 09 92, ☎922 71 10 40. The only accommodation in La Caleta, this unassuming apartment block contains over 200 neat little apartments, sleeping up to three people, that surround a pool and terrace area. €60.

Lagos de Fañabé

C/Londres, Fañabé ☎922 71 25 63, ☎922 71 21 29. Good value one- and two-bedroom apartments (sleeping up to four). Shared facilities include a pleasant garden and somewhat cramped sun decks and pools with chutes and slides to keep kids busy. €60.

Mar y Sol

C/General Franco, Los Cristianos ☎922 79 49 76, ☎922 79 54 73. Unspectacular but well-managed apartment block, thoughtfully developed so all facilities fully accommodate wheelchair users, for which the resident dive school also caters. Both studios and apartments are offered and the complex's facilities include three pools. €144.

Cafés

Cervecería Central

El Camisón, local 17–18, Las Américas. A branch of the classy and popular Santa Cruz café-restaurant, serving everything from coffees and cakes to filled rolls, omelettes and a good variety of tapas. Moderately priced full meals are available in the evenings.

PLACES Los Cristianos, Las Américas and Costa Adeje

Accommodation agencies

Accommodation agencies can help find vacant apartments in large complexes and generally offer a week's rental (usually the minimum booking period) from around €300.

Anyka Sur
Edificio Azahara, Los Cristianos ☎922 79 13 77 or ☎649 40 85 15, ☻www.anykasur.com.

Custom Holidays
Aparthotel California 6, Las Américas ☎922 79 60 00, ☻www.custom-holidays.com.

Marcus Management
Apartamentos Portosin, Avda Penetración, Los Cristianos ☎922 75 10 64, ☻www.canary-isles.com.

Tenerife Holiday Rent
Edificio Tenerife Garden, Las Américas ☎922 79 02 11 or 607 14 66 77, ☻www.tenerife-holiday-rental.com.

Restaurants

Casa del Mar

Esplanada del Muelle, Los Cristianos ☎922 79 32 75. Closed Mon. Large, consistently popular, with a good selection of fish and a terrace overlooking the bay and harbour. Prices are above average but the size and quality of the portions make it good value.

El Caserio

Plaza Las Fuentes, Los Cristianos. Open eves only. Simple Canarian place, combining dim lighting with wooden furniture and offering traditional, inexpensive food, from stews and rabbit to octopus and a decent choice of fish.

Celso

La Caleta. Tues–Sun 12.30–11pm. One of three fish and seafood restaurants gathered around La Caleta's namesake bay. What generally gives the *Celso* the edge over the others are its competitive prices, large patio area and sea views – all of which encourage locals as well as visitors to eat here.

Corisa

C/Antigua General Franco 18, Los Cristianos. Central restaurant with bright lights and vinyl tablecloths. It serves good, reasonably priced fish, seafood and meat dishes – the *menú del día*, which includes wine, is particularly good value.

El Duque

Gran Hotel Bahía del Duque, Fañabé ☎922 71 30 00. Closed Sun & June. One of the most expensive restaurants on the island, this place serves a changing range of international dishes, including the simple but superb house speciality, seafood lasagna. There's also an extensive wine list. Dress is smart casual.

El Gomero

Edificio Las Terrazas. Closed Sun. Speedy service and a menu offering paellas, steaks and cheap but filling set meals are on offer at this straightforward Canarian restaurant.

▼ PUERTO COLÓN

El Gomerón

Edificio Royal, Los Cristianos. Inexpensive eatery with stylish chrome tables, popular with locals for its simple Canarian food, including a decent range of fish and seafood and some good steaks.

Harley's American Diner

Torviscas ☎922 71 30 40. *Harley's* is a fairly expensive theme-bar and restaurant offering a wide range of cocktails and meals, including nachos, fajitas and some vegetarian options. Busy in the evenings, when it's worth booking ahead.

The King And I

Local 12B Garden City, San Eugenio ☎922 75 03 50. Though a little more expensive than the surrounding restaurants, the quality of Thai dishes here – including tasty green curries and a great papaya salad – makes this place worth the extra.

Mamma Rosa

Apartments Colón II, Las Américas ☎922 79 78 23. Smart but expensive Italian restaurant serving delicious pasta and pizza as well as an excellent juicy sirloin steak à la Mamma Rosa – the house speciality.

El Patio Canario

C/Dominguez Alfonso 4, Arona. Closed Sun. Run by a Belgian-Canarian family, this place has good dishes from both culinary traditions and moderate prices.

La Pirámide

Pirámide de Arona, Las Américas ☎922 79 63 60. Daily 7.30–11pm. Gaudy over-the-top decor but superb – if expensive – food and a pleasantly informal atmosphere make this a good choice. Best time to visit is on the thrice-weekly opera night (Tues, Fri & Sat from 8.30pm) when enthusiastic singers perform arias while you eat. A quartet plays chamber music on other nights.

Las Rocas Beach Club

Hotel Jardín Tropical, San Eugenio. Cliff-top beach club where exclusive dining is offered to visitors as well as hotel guests on a terrace overlooking the sea. The restaurant specializes in rice and seafood dishes – particularly recommended are the paellas, including a vegetarian version.

Rincón del Mero

Esplanada del Muelle, Los Cristianos ☎922 79 35 53. Functional restaurant with moderate prices where only fresh fish and seafood grace the menu.

Los Spaghetto

CC San Telmo, Los Cristianos. Daily 11am–1am. Small Italian restaurant with views over the beach and phenomenal, moderately priced home-made pasta. Leave space for the fabulous Tiramisu, too.

Bars

Dubliner

Hotel Las Palmeras, Las Américas. Dependable source of good *craic*, with an enthusiastic live band playing a mix of vaguely contemporary hits to a large, mixed-age crowd. Busiest between 10pm and 4am.

Harry's Bar

Plaza de Américas, Las Américas. Small, swanky bar, done out in an African theme in the shadow of *Mare Nostrum*'s pyramid.

Lineker's Bar

CC Starco, Las Américas. Fun party atmosphere in a bar owned by former England footballer Gary Lineker and run by his brother. It tends to get going earlier (around 10pm) than those over the road at CC Veronicas.

Clubs

Bobby's

CC Las Veronicas, Las Américas. Thanks to exposure in a TV docusoap, this dark, first-floor club is the most famous in Veronicas. It shares a landing with the similar *Busby's* and both get busy from about 2am, pumping out run of the mill dance music.

Metropolis

Beside Hotel Conquistador, Las Américas. Large club, packed and fun at weekends and almost exclusively patronized by Canarians.

Shows

Moonlight Fun Pub

Pueblo Torviscas. Consistently popular place drawing a mixed-age crowd to its seafront location. Cheesy nightly shows feature Billy Idol and Tina Turner lookalikes.

Pirámide de Arona

Mare Nostrum Resort ☎922 79 63 60. Flamboyant shows including reasonable flamenco, occasional ballet and the odd theatre performance. Tickets bought through agents and hotels are frequently cheaper than those at the venue.

Tropicana

Costa Adeje ☎902 33 12 34, ✉reservas@tropicanaatlantico.co. Tues, Thurs & Sat. Dinner 8pm, show 9pm. €45 including drinks, €52 including meal and drinks. Vivacious Cuban dance show followed by an after midnight disco for up to 1500 that has a huge following among the local Canarian populace.

The south coast

Tenerife's **south coast** is where mass tourism on the island began. Built in the 1960s, the vast *Ten-Bel* hotel complex, beside the small workaday town of Las Galletas, was one of the first large-scale holiday centres, and the bland Costa del Silencio resort has grown up beside it. East of here is the Golf del Sur, a new resort centred on two large golf courses, while further east still is the most picturesque town along this stretch of coast, **El Médano**, whose vast, windswept beaches are the only significant natural ones on the island. The monotony of the landscape is broken by a number of hills – Rasca in the west and Roja and Pelada in the east – that are designated nature reserves, offering opportunities for hiking and mountain-biking. Down on the coast, meanwhile, numerous diving concerns operate out of Las Galletas and El Médano.

Las Galletas and the Costa del Silencio

Bus #115 from Santa Cruz, 4–12 daily, 1hr 10min; #467 or #473 from Los Cristianos and Las Américas, very frequent, 45min; and #473 from Los Gigantes, very frequent, 1hr 40min.

Though largely given over to the tourist industry, Las Galletas still has the feel of a small coastal town with a handful of shops, bars and restaurants along its main pedestrian street and the short seafront promenade. Here you'll find a narrow pebble beach, where waves crashing along the rocky shoreline attract local surfers and body-boarders.

Eastern Las Galletas merges into the Costa del Silencio, an ironic name given that it

▲ THE COSTA DEL SILENCIO

Information

Las Galletas' tourist information booth (Mon–Fri 9am–1pm & 4–7pm, Sat 9am–1pm; ☎922 73 01 33) is on pedestrianized La Rambla, behind the seafront promenade. In El Médano, the helpful tourist information booth (Mon–Fri 9am–1pm & 4–7pm, Sat 9am–1pm; ☎922 17 60 02) is on the north side of Plaza Principe de Asturias.

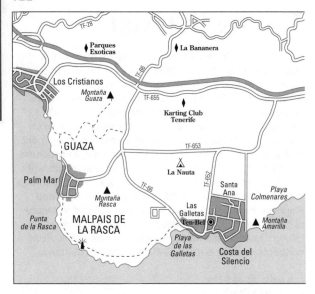

consists of a couple of kilometres of almost uninterrupted development along a slim spit of shingle beach, with numerous expat businesses in charmless commercial centres.

Malpais de la Rasca hike

12km/3–4hr from Las Galletas to Los Cristianos, returning on bus #467 or #473 (very frequent, 45min).

Following the rugged coastline west of Las Galletas through the wild natural landscape of Malpais de la Rasca, this hike gives a glimpse of how things looked along the coast here before tourism took over. The route is virtually shadeless, so bring plenty of suncream and water.

From Las Galletas, head west along the promenade beside the shingle beach. At its end, and by a Red Cross building, turn left onto a rough, unsigned coastal path. The path is crisscrossed by many others but as long as you keep the

coastline in sight, which one you follow doesn't matter. After half an hour's walk you arrive first at a disused plantation and then at a working one, a clear path passing each on the ocean side. Beyond the second plantation the Faro de Rasca lighthouse comes into view and you enter the protected reserve area. Follow the obvious track to the lighthouse and then beyond – turning inland for around 100m on an asphalt road before joining a dirt road just in front of it. Around ten minutes beyond the lighthouse, ignore a path that heads right in the direction of Montaña Rasca and continue straight on, only to bear right at the next fork shortly after. The following fork is beside a low wall – bear left here on a track to an abandoned house, then continue on a path that begins behind the building. Passing some disused fields and a low wall, head for the coastal fortification in the fledgling resort

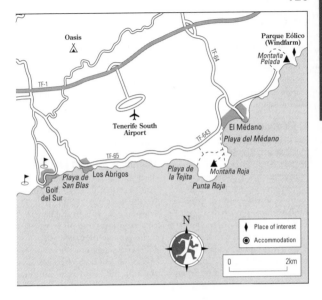

of Palm Mar. From the
fortification continue to the far
side of the bay where a steep path
starts to climb between cliffs. The
path is marked with a sign
announcing the protected area of
Guaza and is soon indistinct as it
clambers steeply up the rock. Bear
slightly left as you head up and
you'll see a clear path resuming a
zig-zag progress up the hill – again
bear left at all junctions. Once up
on the plateau the coastal path is
easily spotted as it dips in and out
of several dry gorges. Finally, with
views of eastern Los Cristianos
visible below, you come to a steep
gorge where the path becomes
indistinct. Here the choice is to
either head inland, cross-country
to the clear wide track that heads
up Guaza – an extra 20min walk
– or to clamber down the gorge
and on into Los Cristianos. Once
in the town it's a one-kilometre
walk along the promenade to the
bus station and services back to
Las Galletas.

Montaña Amarilla

East of Costa del Silencio, the
unspoilt protected lands around
Montaña Amarilla contain a
wild and rugged coastline. The
short ascent of the hill itself is
worth it for the view over both

▼ MONTAÑA AMARILLA

the resort and a rocky piece of scrub where cacti thrive. The striking twisted forms and a sheltered bay around its base are equally alluring, with ladders giving access to turquoise waters, in which it's generally safe to swim.

El Médano

Bus #116 from Santa Cruz, 8 daily, 1hr; from Los Cristianos and Las Américas, 16 daily, 50min. Best known for its sandy beaches and breezy conditions – great for wind- and kite-surfing, not so good for sunbathing – the small town of El Médano has developed into a laid-back resort for sporty types. Though it hasn't escaped the region's on-going building boom, it has managed to retain a pleasant easy-going atmosphere. The town centres on **Plaza Principe de Asturias**, surrounded by restaurants and cafés and adjacent to the large main beach. From here a boardwalk follows the length of the natural stretch of sand, lined with shops selling clothing and watersports paraphernalia.

Montañas Roja and Pelada

Two distinctive hills of twisted volcanic rock flank El Médano. To the west the 171-metre Montaña Roja is in the centre of a nature reserve protecting a dune ecosystem. One easily followed path from the western end of El Médano's beach leads through this area to the summit,

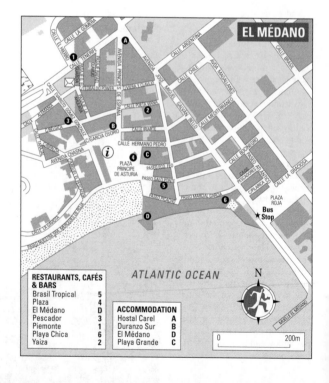

EL MÉDANO

ATLANTIC OCEAN

N

RESTAURANTS, CAFÉS & BARS	
Brasil Tropical	5
Plaza	4
El Médano	D
Pescador	3
Piemonte	1
Playa Chica	6
Yaiza	2

ACCOMMODATION	
Hostal Carel	A
Duranzo Sur	B
El Médano	D
Playa Grande	C

0   200m

▲ MONTAÑA ROJA

while another rounds the hill on its inland side and leads to a beautiful but windswept beach, **Playa de la Tejita**.

To the east of town, along a dirt road that follows the coast, is the magnificent crater of Montaña Pelada, shaped by an influx of seawater during a volcanic eruption. A **hiking trail** begins from the eastern end of the coastal road from El Médano before dropping into a sheltered sandy bay – popular with nudists – before heading up a steep, unmarked route to the crater rim, from where there are good views along the coast. You can follow a trail around the crater rim, returning back down the steep west side, or descend on its northern side to link up with a track that leads east to the Parque Eólico. The eight-kilometre return hike to the Parque Eólico from El Médano takes around three hours.

Parque Eólico

☎922 39 10 00, ext.62, ⓦwww.iter.es. Mon–Fri 10am–5pm. Free. Signposted Pol. Industrial Granadilla. An innovative wind farm and renewable energy centre, the Parque Eólico offers visitors a trip along an ecological walkway lined with entertaining exhibits demonstrating principles behind solar and wind power. The topic of domestic power consumption is examined in the "bioclimatic dwellings" – several examples of energy-efficient homes – on the coast below the wind farm.

Hotels

El Médano

Playa del Médano ☎922 17 70 00, ⓦwww.medano.es. Sixties hotel, built on stilts over the sea, catering largely for package tourists and not as luxurious as it once was. However, it's in a superb central location and many of the rooms have excellent views. €60.

▼ PARQUE EÓLICO

Playa Sur Tenerife

Playa del Médano ☎922 17 61 20, ⊛www.hotelplayasurtenerife.com. Modern, package-oriented hotel west of the centre at the end of the boardwalk. The seventy rooms are elegantly furnished and the hotel has all the usual four-star facilities, plus some outdoor activities, including hiking. €70.

Pensions

Hostal Carel

Avda. Principes de España 22, El Médano ☎922 17 60 66. Simply furnished but clean singles and doubles – some with private bathrooms – in a renovated pension on the edge of the town centre, beside the main approach road. €35.

Pension La Estrella

Avda. del Atlantico, km 1, Las Galletas ☎922 73 15 62. A kilometre inland from Las Galletas and on a busy road, this place offers a mix of rooms, some en suite and all at reasonable rates. €23.

▾ SOUTH COAST KITESURFERS

Pension Los Vinitos

C/Venezuela 4, Las Galletas ☎922 78 58 03. The smarter of the two simply decorated and reliable pensions in Las Galletas, the rooms here are a little less cramped and each has a private bath. Some singles too. €22.

Apartments

Bungalows Ker Tulakito

La Gaviota 17, El Médano ☎922 17 70 83. Pretty, well-equipped bungalows, with excellent views over the bay, five minutes west of the town centre. Each has its own garden and terrace and sleeps up to four. The friendly owner speaks English. €60.

Duranzo Sur

Avda. Principes de España 1, El Médano ☎922 17 69 58, ⊕922 17 62 99. Unusually spacious and simply equipped apartments, many of which have balconies overlooking the main plaza and the sea. Most sleep up to three, but there are singles too. English spoken. €50.

Playa Grande

C/Hermano Pedro 2, El Médano ☎922 17 63 06, ⊕922 17 61 68. Swish, modern apartments overlooking the main plaza and sleeping up to four. Along with Scandinavian-style furnishings, they all have telephones, satellite TV, a balcony and access to a roof terrace. €50.

Ten-Bel

Avda. del Atlántico, Las Galletas ☎922 73 07 21, ⊛www.tenbel.com. The area's original holiday village has stood the test of time surprisingly well. The 4500-bed complex offers everything from simple studios to apartments sleeping up to seven, most with balconies and some overlooking the sea. Communal facilities include

Acccommodation agencies

Trading Post
La Rambla 8, Las Galletas ☎922 73 00 58. Accommodation agency, near the tourist-office booth. Apartments from €250 per week.

tennis courts and a large salt-water pool by a tiny beach. €30.

Camping

Camping La Nauta

On TF-653, 2km inland of Las Galletas, just off the road to Guaza ☎922 78 51 18. One of the island's few campsites, this place has worn facilities including a swimming pool and rudimentary sports area. The tent sites (€4 per person) are dusty and uninviting, but most of the site is given over to basic cabins sleeping up to four (€18).

Oasis

Ciguaña Alta; signposted off a small road off the northern side of the airport motorway junction: Autopista Sur, exit 22 ☎922 77 04 14. Small, neat and simple campsite with great views over the coast and friendly owners. Its one drawback is its relative isolation – about 3km from the nearest public transport. Daily charges are €2 each per tent, person and car.

Cafés

Flashpoint

Playa del Médano. Overlooking the beach at the western end of town, this trendy café with a shady terrace serves excellent breakfasts and filled rolls and pizzas in the afternoon. In the evening the bar takes over, serving drinks and snacks against a drum'n'bass soundtrack.

Plaza

Plaza Principe de Asturias, El Médano. Popular café taking up one end of the town's main plaza, offering plenty of outdoor seating and views over the sea.

Los Vinitos

C/Venezuela, Las Galletas. One of a number of cafés along the town's pedestrianized street and as good a place as any to head for snacks and light lunches. Along with the budget sandwiches, hamburgers and omelettes, there's also a good range of tapas and fresh-pressed juices.

Restaurants

L'Alpage

La Estrella 7, Las Galletas ☎922/730 577. Closed Sun. Excellent Swiss restaurant, sporting heavy alpine furnishings and red-check tablecloths. It's a bit of a trek out of town – 1km past *Ten Bel* along Avenida del Atlántico – but worth it for the wonderful fondue and rösti dishes at moderate prices.

Carnaval

Paseo Marítima, Las Galletas. A dimly lit and atmospheric place in a strip of otherwise functional seafood restaurants. Salads, hamburgers and sandwiches are served for lunch, while the reasonably priced and varied dinner menu includes seafood and more unusual offerings such as ostrich.

Colibri Playa

Paseo Maritima, Las Galletas. Popular with locals, this basic restaurant has one of the largest and least expensive menus of fish and seafood in town. The menu varies according to the day's catch, but portions are always generous.

El Médano

Hotel El Médano, Plaza Principe de Asturias, El Médano. Though the salads, meats and vegetables at this nightly buffet are far from exciting, the views over the sea couldn't be better, and the prices are very reasonable.

Pescador

C/Evarvisto Gómez Gonzalez 15, El Médano. Closed Tues. Popular with locals, this restaurant serves reliably good, moderately priced fresh fish and seafood dishes at tables decked with cheerful green cloths.

Piemonte

C/Gran Canaria 7, El Médano. Closed Wed & Sat eve. Tucked away in a basement on the edge of the town centre, this stylish, pastel-toned Italian restaurant offers a large menu of top-quality pizza and pasta dishes at above average prices.

Playa Chica

Paseo Marcial García, El Médano. Closed Mon. Inexpensive tapas and fine views over the bay from the downstairs terrace make this a popular place for a snack; the restaurant upstairs is also good value, serving the usual fish and meat dishes.

Vista Mar

Los Abrigos, 6km west of El Médano. The town of Los Abrigos has a reputation as an outstanding place to eat fresh fish and seafood, and the *Vista Mar* has one of the best selections. Other options include *La Langostera*, a lobster specialist, the more gourmet *Bencomo*, or the cheap and simple *Yaisara*, which also offers a good range of salads.

Yaiza

C/Iriarte 12, El Médano. Closed Thurs. Elegant restaurant serving creative, expensive gourmet food. The menu includes interesting fish dishes, such as sole in saffron sauce, and various choice cuts of meat – but no vegetarian options.

Bars

Brasil Tropical

Paseo Galo Ponte, El Médano. Snazzy cocktails served in a lively tropical-style bar, just off Principe de Asturias. Open till 2am, this is usually one of the last places in town to close.

Paropo

C/La Arena, Las Galletas. Of several places in the area this is the pick of the bunch – a small, smoky and atmospheric bar where locals congregate to watch sport on TV and eat tapas.

Peanut Disco Bar

CC El Chapparal, Costa del Silencio. Sociable pub offering a little more atmosphere than the glut of places over the road in the CC Trebol.

Clubs

Disco Lord

CC El Chapparal. Closed Tues & Wed. Pumping out the usual array of chart music and also hosting Sixties and Seventies nights, the area's single, low-key, disco is nothing special.

Teide and the interior

Set inside an enormous crater at the centre of the island, the **Parque Nacional Las Cañadas del Teide** dominates a bleak and sun-baked volcanic desert. Used as a set for *Star Wars*, the harsh landscape is often familiar to many of the 3.5 million annual visitors, many of whom come to take the cable-car up **Pico del Teide** (3718m), the colossal peak at its heart. One of the highest volcanoes in the world, Teide rises from the lava and pumice plains of Las Cañadas to cast the world's largest shadow over the surrounding ocean and form one of the most enduring symbols of the island. The park is also of considerable interest for its endemic flora, spectacular examples of which occur in May or June when the resilient Teide violet provides a scattering of colour, while the two-metre-high conical Tajinaste rojo blooms with beautiful maroon flowers.

A single east–west road crosses the park with numerous stops providing views of the park and access to walking routes that allow a closer look at the scenery, some of which is only reachable on foot. If you plan to hike, take plenty of sunscreen and water, and don't leave anything on display in a parked car – theft from vehicles is a common problem.

With little accommodation in the park itself, a tranquil and practical upland base is the traditional village of **Vilaflor**, Spain's highest settlement, located at the edge of the Canarian pine forest and in sight of some of its largest specimens.

Vilaflor

Bus #482 from Los Cristianos, 3 daily, 1hr 15min. With incredible views, pure upland air and local springs, it's easy to see how this former spa town's charming old brick-and-tile houses once attracted those looking to improve their health. Though less busy nowadays, the town retains something of its appeal with a friendly, traditionally Canarian atmosphere. The main street, Calle Santo Domingo, heads up to a large plaza with the plain but imposing seventeenth-century Iglesia de San Pedro at its heart. From the plaza it's a short, steep walk up to the viewpoint, Mirador San Roque (just west of the road to Teide), which provides a spectacular view over the slopes of southern Tenerife.

Paisaje Lunar hike

6km/2–3hr beginning 9km northeast of Vilaflor or 14km/6hr return hike from Vilaflor. One of the best hikes you can do through the Canarian pine forest goes to the Paisaje Lunar – a moonscape of

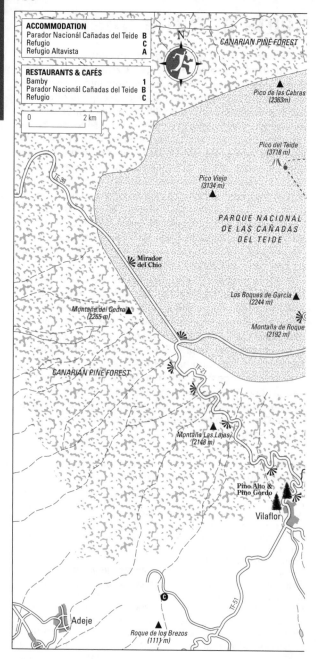

ACCOMMODATION

Parador Naciónal Cañadas del Teide	B
Refugio	C
Refugio Altavista	A

RESTAURANTS & CAFÉS

Bamby	1
Parador Naciónal Cañadas del Teide	B
Refugio	C

0   2 km

CANARIAN PINE FOREST

Pico de las Cabras (2363m)

Pico del Teide (3718 m)

Pico Viejo (3134 m)

PARQUE NACIONAL DE LAS CAÑADAS DEL TEIDE

Mirador del Chio

Los Roques de García (2244 m)

Montaña del Cedro (2265 m)

Montaña de Roque (2192 m)

TF-38

TF-21

CANARIAN PINE FOREST

Montaña Las Lajas (2148 m)

Pino Alto & Pino Gordo

Vilaflor

TF-51

Adeje

Roque de los Brezos (111 m)

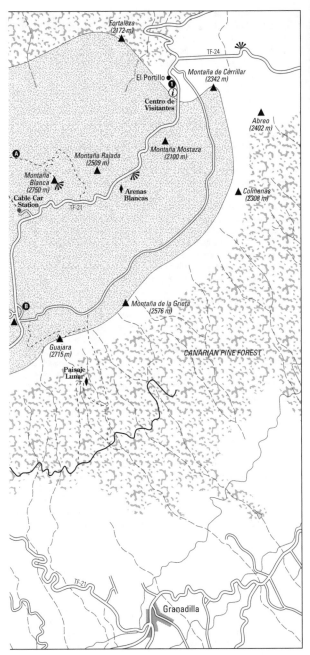

Arrival and information

It's easiest to get to the national park by **car**, though there are daily **buses** from Las Américas and Los Cristianos (#342, 1 daily, 1hr 40min) and from Puerto de la Cruz (#348, 1 daily, 1hr 45min) calling at the *Parador*, the base of the cable-car, and the visitors' centre.

Of the four routes to the park the **road from the west** is the fastest. Beginning its ascent near Santiago del Teide, it climbs through a thin belt of pines, passing south of an area of solidified lava from the most recent (1909) eruption of Montaña Chinyero. Beyond the trees the road rises through twisted lava formations, created when the side vent, Las Narices del Teide (Teide's Nostrils), spewed twelve million cubic metres of molten rock in 1789. The vent is technically part of Pico Viejo (3134m), a peak in its own right that rises out from the side of Teide.

From the south a busier road climbs to the national park via Vilaflor and through impressive stands of Canarian pines, with good views over southern Tenerife and La Gomera.

Coming **from the east** visitors take the relatively long and impressive route along the **Cumbre Dorsal**, the mountain backbone of the island. Climbing quickly through La Esperanza, the road ascends through some of the largest sections of pine forest on the island with a number of viewpoints. Once past the trees the route passes the **Izaña Observatory**, home to the Instituto Astrofísica de Canarias (🌐).

The busy **road from the north** twists around countless hairpins before rising into the dense vegetation on the damp side of the island, where low cloud often obscures the views.

The main **visitors' centre** (daily 9am–4pm; ☎922 29 01 29) is at the eastern end of the park and has displays on geology, flora and fauna, plus maps and leaflets about the generally well-marked hiking trails. The centre also organizes free **guided hikes** of varying difficulty. There's a second centre (same hours) beside the *Parador* on the south side of the park that concentrates on the park's human heritage. Lastly, two tiny booths, with unpredictable opening hours, field general enquiries and distribute leaflets: one is at the junction of the roads from the west and the south, the other at the junction of the roads from the east and north.

eroded rock that comprises two small areas of tall, thin and smooth rock columns.

The dirt road to the trailhead is marked by a wooden sign on a bend in the road to the Parque Nacional, not far above Vilaflor. From here it's a two-hour walk, or half-hour drive to the trail proper. The road is hard on cars – if you're in a rental, check that your insurance covers you off sealed roads.

Marked by white-painted rocks, the hike from the dirt road to the columns begins on a narrow woodland trail, but the trees soon thin out to reveal good views of Tenerife's southern coast 17km away and the ridge-like rim of the vast Las Cañadas crater 2km ahead. After 3km you arrive at the first of the Paisaje Lunar's columns, eroded stone whose wide bases support tapering pillars with delicate looking, top-heavy tips. A clear trail runs past them turning downhill and southeast to the second group across an area of volcanic ash. From here an obvious path continues down, following the contours of the hill and some water pipes, before dropping into a children's summer camp. Take the dirt

▲ LOS ROQUES DE GARCIA

track at its base, which leads to dirt road back to Vilaflor – bear right to get to the start point about 1km away.

Los Roques de García hike

3.5km/1hr–1hr 30min circular hike.
The best short hike in the centre of the national park loops around the bizarre and twisted Roques de García, a line of huge rocks that serve as a reminder of the erosive forces that helped shape the park. Formed from magma forced through near-vertical underground cracks, Los Roques are volcanic dykes that solidified into walls of stone.

Much harder than the surrounding rock, this cooled magma has remained while the softer surrounding material has eroded away. Where softer rock forms a horizontal layer near the base, a top-heavy structure like the **Roque Cinchado** – a precariously balanced formation – emerges.

The route that takes in these formations is best done anti-clockwise, heading out of the car park beside Roque Cinchado in the direction of Teide then following a well-trodden path to the northernmost rock in the line

The Canarian pine forest

The grand forest of Canarian pines that all but encircles the Parque Nacional begins just north of Vilaflor and it's here that the biggest specimens are found including one, Pino Gordo (Fat Pine) with a trunk circumference of 9.3m and, opposite, Pino Alto (Tall Pine), the highest on the island at almost 50m.

If the proportions of the Canarian pine are impressive, then the species' characteristics are even more so, showing how well it has adapted to its environment.

Long needles trap moisture from the clouds, introducing vital water into the island's arid ecosystem, while to stop other species from taking advantage of this, the needles degrade slowly and have an acidifying effect on the soil, meaning little else can grow. The tree has also developed a mechanism for dealing with the fires that are common on volcanic islands: a thick bark that protects the tree's heart from the flames making it common to see badly scorched trees sprouting healthy new branches.

▲ GUAJARA

before dipping to follow a rougher trail back down the other side of the landforms. The final section of the route passes the massive rock monolith, **La Catedral**, with its striking geometric patterns, before returning steeply back to the car park.

Guajara hike

5km/4hr circular hike. Part of the ancient crater rim that forms the park boundary, **Guajara** (2715m) stands over 700m above the crater floor, from where it looks more like a series of cliff faces than a mountain.

Though a fairly strenuous hike, it's without a doubt one of the best walks on the island. The path climbing across its sheer north face has excellent views over the whole national park and is a good perspective from which to make out the most recent lava tongues on the slopes of Teide, while on clear days the panorama at the summit includes La Gomera, La Palma, El Hierro and Gran Canaria.

The trail begins just a few metres south of the *Parador* beside a sign depicting park footpaths. The narrow track soon ends in a T-junction, where a left turn follows a path that curves to the right before meeting a road (there are parking spaces here too). Across the road, the reasonably well-trodden trail heads straight up, marked by occasional paint spots. Around 500m beyond the road the path bears left and begins to steepen as it crosses the base of a cliff face and leads out onto the crater rim. From this point the route steepens further, leading up to the foot of a row of cliffs that mark Guajara's northern face. The path climbs beside, and then passes over, the cliffs (follow the irregular and faded paint

Las Cañadas geology

At only 3 million years old, the area protected by the national park is in the youngest part of Tenerife, having joined up the older volcanic ranges to the north, west and south to form a large island backbone, the **Cumbre Dorsal**. Volcanic activity in the centre of the island reached a peak around 300,000 years ago in a volcano of spectacular proportions whose sixteen-kilometre-wide crater now forms the boundary of today's park. Exactly what geological event destroyed this volcano is unclear – subsequent eruptions and thousands of years of erosion make it difficult to tell – but the crater rim is still clear in the south of the park where the steep-sided mountain of **Guajara** is its highest point.

The summit permit

Only **150 visitors a day** are allowed up to the eight-metre wide crater rim on the summit of Teide and the tiny sulphurous vents that surround it. To get one of the free permits, apply in person with your passport and a photocopy of the photo and details page at the **ICONA park administration** in Santa Cruz (C/Emilio Calzadilla 5; Mon–Fri 9am–2pm; ☎922 29 01 29). You need to book the time you'll be visiting the top, but it's generally OK if you turn up outside this time, though you may have to wait if there are people on the summit. Note that if there's snow, the peak closes to visitors.

markings carefully to find the quickest way to the summit), past a triangulation point to the summit and a large wind shelter. The descent is to the east of here – paths to the south lead in the direction of Vilaflor and Paisaje Lunar, but to return to Las Cañadas continue along the line of the crater rim. This path, which is steep and loose with small pumice rocks, heads down to a saddle just over a kilometre away where it's crossed by another path. From here you have two options: head north around 500m back downhill to reach the crater floor and follow the wide track along the base of Guajara back to the *Parador*; or right at this junction will take you south to Paisaje Lunar from where you can easily hike to Vilaflor, in around three hours (13km; see p.129).

Teide by cable car

☎922 37 46 69. Daily 9am–4pm. €18 return, €11 one-way. Not for those with vertigo, the ride up Teide by cable car is nonetheless one of the most spectacular eight-minute journeys you can make anywhere. Following a near-vertical, thousand-metre climb, the trip affords spectacular views back down the side of the mountain and around Las Cañadas, before depositing passengers 200m below the summit. From here two easy walks lead to two **viewpoints**, giving the best views of the park, island and entire archipelago (on a really good day). Permit holders (see above) can, of course, make the short steep climb to the summit of Teide (around 30min one-way). High winds, snow and occasional maintenance can close the cable car at short

▼THE SUMMIT

notice so if in doubt, call ahead. In summer, it's also worth getting here as early as possible, as substantial queues soon build up. Be sure to bring plenty of warm clothes too, as temperatures at the summit often hover around freezing.

Teide on foot

12km/7–8hr return hike. An alternative to the cable car and the obvious challenge for fit visitors is the hugely strenuous ascent of Teide on foot. The hike up takes around four hours, with another three needed for the descent – though many hikers catch the cable car to save their joints the strain of the descent. There is only one permissible route up the peak, obvious from the summit of Montaña Blanca (see p.137), which quickly becomes rough, narrow and steep as it zigzags its way up the solidified lava flows on Teide's flanks. There are no real landmarks in this desolate landscape and few distractions from the gruelling climb, so the *Refugio Altavista* (☎922 23 98 11; €12 per person; closed Nov–Feb), an hour and a half's hike beyond Montaña Blanca, is a welcome sight. Reservations are advsiable if you plan to stay here and though there are some cooking facilities, water can be in short supply so bring plenty of your own, plus a sleeping bag to combat the low night temperatures. From the *refugio* it's roughly another hour straight climb to the top through a similar craggy area, though the grade of ascent begins to ease. After around twenty minutes a short detour is possible (marked by a pile of stones) to the Cueva del Hielo (Ice Cave), where a slippery metal ladder leads down into a small cavern in which numerous stalactites grow. From the turn off it's another thirty minutes' walk to the top cable-car station. It you have permission (see p.135) to ascend to the summit, follow the obvious stone path near the cable-car station to the pale sulphurous pit that constitutes the volcano's crater from where you'll have unrivalled views over the island and, in all likelihood, the entire Canarian archipelago. Note that the high altitude of Teide means lower concentrations of oxygen which make altitude sickness, in the form of a headache or dizziness, common. Slowing the pace is usually enough to solve such problems but if this doesn't work then you need to head back down.

▾ TAJINASTE ROJO

Montaña Blanca hike

6km/2hr return hike.

Beginning at a roadside car park, 4km east of the cable car station, Montaña Blanca (2740m) is a great destination in itself, though for many hikers it's just a stop on the way to or from Teide. The path up is well graded and wide, and takes in vast swathes of beige pumice gravel dotted with huge dark, lava boulders, their shape earning them the name Huevos de Teide (Teide's Eggs). The mountain's smooth rounded summit is a particularly good place to enjoy the sunset (after which there's just enough time to get back down before dark) when the immense, triangular shadow of Teide covers the valley floor.

▲ PINO ALTO

Hotels

Alta Montaña

C/Morro del Cano 1, Vilaflor ☎922 70 90 00. Just outside the centre of Vilaflor across the Teide road, this stylish hotel has en-suite double and single rooms, a garden with a swimming pool and splendid coastal views. €42.

Parador Naciónal de Cañadas del Teide

Parque Nacional Las Cañadas del Teide ☎922 38 64 15 or 922 37 48 41, ⊛www.parador.es. Stylish, state-run hotel in a fantastic and unique location in the national park. All the rooms have great views and there's a small pool, sauna, lounge and restaurant. €85.

El Sombrerito

C/Santa Catalina 15, Vilaflor ☎922 70 90 52. Smart but simple hotel in the centre of Vilaflor. Rooms here are all en suite and some have a balcony overlooking the quiet main street. €40.

Pensions

Pension German

C/Santo Domingo 1, Vilaflor ☎922 70 90 28. Friendly, well-run pension in the centre of Vilaflor, with clean inexpensive rooms – some with private bathroom – including some singles. €30.

Refugio

Close to Ifonche ☎922 72 58 94. Only a practical option if you have your own transport, this B&B is in a small house by the road to Ifonche, west off the Arona–Vilaflor road. It has stupendous views over the coast, simple rooms and is run by keen hikers and paragliders, who are happy to advise (in English) about local routes and conditions. €50.

▲ LAS CAÑADAS

Restaurants

Bamby

El Portillo. A large outdoor terrace with splendid views over Teide makes this the best of three restaurants – all bus-tour favourites – near the visitor centre in the hamlet of El Portillo. Average Canarian food at reasonable prices.

El Mirador

Mirador San Roque, Vilaflor ☎922 70 91 35. Vilaflor's best restaurant, just below the viewpoint, isn't too pricey, considering the grand views and the quality of the Canarian and international cuisine available.

Parador Nacionál de Cañadas del Teide

Parque Nacional Las Cañadas del Teide ☎922 38 64 15 or 922 37 48 41. Large and expensive restaurant with a rather sterile atmosphere, but serving good Canarian cuisine and a particularly tasty local stew (*puchero*). The hotel also contains an overpriced café and a lovely bar that's ideal for a celebratory drink after a hike.

Pension German

C/Santo Domingo 1, Vilaflor. Inexpensive restaurant in one of the town's pensions, good for typically hearty upland Canarian fare, like the thick vegetable stew, *escaldón*.

Refugio

Ifonche ☎922 72 58 94. Closed Wed, Sat & Sun. If you have your own transport, try the rustic restaurant at this small house-cum-pension. There's a limited range of tasty, though relatively expensive, home-made dishes, including great *gazpacho*, and fantastic views over the coast from the patio.

San Sebastián and around

La Gomera's busiest transport hub, **San Sebastián**, was the first Spanish settlement on the island and is now its capital and largest town, with a population of just 5000. Central to the town's role is its sheltered harbour, home to yachts and ferries from Tenerife. The harbour also witnessed La Gomera's most famous hour when, on September 6, 1492, Christopher Columbus left here on his first voyage to the Americas – an event with which all of the town's modest sights emphasize their connections. Most buildings have been destroyed and rebuilt several times since then, following repeated pirate attacks, but the old streets are worth a visit, as are the town's sandy beaches.

Most visitors soon move on to quieter parts of the island, but San Sebastián is easily the island's most practical base. All island bus and ferry routes radiate from here and the selection of bars and restaurants makes it a fine place to retire to after a day in the mountains or at the resort of **Playa de Santiago**, a few kilometres southwest. And with mass tourism almost entirely absent, it's also a great place to sample small-town Canarian life.

Casa Aduana

Plaza de la Constitución. Mon–Fri 9am–1.30pm, Sat & Sun 10am–1pm. Free. The seventeenth-century Casa Aduana (Customs House) houses the town's tourist office and a couple of rooms displaying information about Columbus's voyage to the Americas. Scale models of his three ships are worth a look, but the most famous connection with the explorer, in the courtyard of the building, is the Pozo de la Aguada, the well from which Columbus took his water supplies to subsequently "baptize" the New World.

Arrival and information

San Sebastián is connected to Tenerife by three **ferry companies**, one of which operates a passenger service on to Playa de Santiago and Valle Gran Rey (see p.144 & 148). The town's **tourist office** (Mon–Fri 9am–1.30pm, Sat & Sun 10am–1pm; ☎922 14 01 47) is in the old Customs House, on the corner of C/del Medio and Plaza de la Constitución. There's also a much smaller office on Playa de Santiago's Avda. Maritima (Mon–Fri 10am–2pm; ☎922 87 02 81).

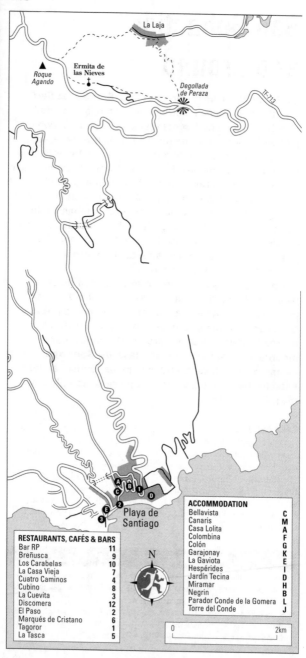

La Laja

Roque Agando

Ermita de las Nieves

Degollada de Peraza

TF-713

Playa de Santiago

N

ACCOMMODATION

Bellavista	C
Canaris	M
Casa Lolita	A
Colombina	F
Colón	G
Garajonay	K
La Gaviota	E
Hespérides	I
Jardín Tecina	D
Miramar	H
Negrin	B
Parador Conde de la Gomera	L
Torre del Conde	J

RESTAURANTS, CAFÉS & BARS

Bar RP	11
Breñusca	9
Los Carabelas	10
La Casa Vieja	7
Cuatro Caminos	4
Cubino	8
La Cuevita	3
Discomera	12
El Paso	2
Marqués de Cristano	6
Tagoror	1
La Tasca	5

0   2km

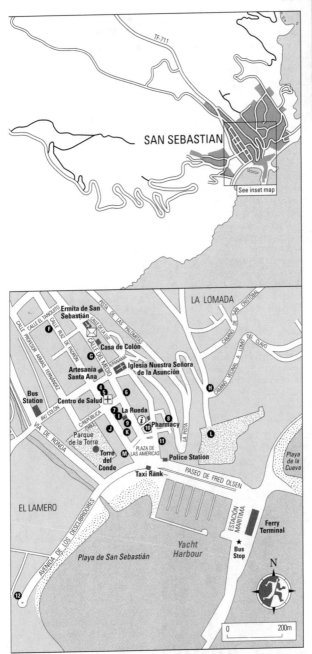

Torre del Conde

Tues–Sat 10am–1pm. Free. San Sebastián's first building of any note was the stocky medieval Torre del Conde fort, built in 1447 as a strategic fall-back during the slow conquest of the island. It proved useful, serving its purpose when Beatriz de Bobadilla, the wife of the murdered governor Hernán Peraza, barricaded herself in during a 1488 uprising until help arrived. Today the fort contains displays on Gomeran history with maps from 1492 showing how, at the time when Columbus was striking out into unknown waters, most of the Gomeran interior was still uncharted – and would remain so until the seventeenth century. A copy of the 1743 demand by English naval officer Charles Windham, ordering that San Sebastián give up arms and surrender, is also here, along with the defiant reply of Diego Bueno, representative of the citizens of San Sebastián, and a print of the subsequent British retreat.

▼ TORRE DEL CONDE

Iglesia Nuestra Señora de la Asunción

C/del Medio. Mass Mon, Wed, Fri & Sun 11am & 1pm. Before setting off on his voyage, Columbus supposedly visited the town's main church for a final session of prayers. Construction of the building started in 1490 and took twenty years to complete, so it's difficult to imagine what it would have looked like in 1492. In any case, an attack by Algerian pirates in 1618 destroyed all but its basic structure, so today's church dates mostly from the seventeenth century – a brick-and-lime, mostly Gothic-style construction, with some Baroque elements, particularly in the carvings of the impressive wooden altars. A large faded mural on one wall of the church depicts the successful repulse of Windham's naval attack on the island (see Torre Del Conde, left), cause for great celebration in a town weary of rebuilding after repeated pirate attacks. The archway to the left of the main entrance is called the Puerta del Perdón which the Guanches were invited to step through for a full amnesty after their 1488 uprising. Hundreds came only to find they had been tricked and be either executed or sold as slaves.

Casa de Colón

C/del Medio 56. Mon–Fri 9am–1pm, 4.30–7.30pm, Sat 9am–1pm. Free. A quaint, wooden-balconied seventeenth-century house, the so-called Casa de Colón (Columbus's House) was actually built over a hundred years after the explorer's death. Even so, maps of the voyage, pieces of Peruvian pottery, and small rotating exhibitions of contemporary Gomeran art are worth a visit.

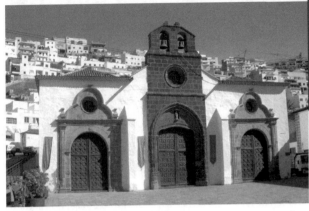

▲ IGLESIA NUESTRA SEÑORA DE LA ASUNCIÓN

Ermita de San Sebastián

C/del Medio. Built in 1450, the tiny Ermita de San Sebastián was the island's first chapel, but, like most buildings in the town, it was not spared by marauding pirates who destroyed it three times. Recent restoration has returned the building to its original form. One of the few decorations on

▼ CASA DE COLÓN

display – fourteen iron crosses on the wall – represent the Stations of the Cross.

Playa de San Sebastián and Playa de la Cueva

San Sebastián's central plazas overlook the bay, harbour and a promenade beside the island's longest (400m) sandy beach, Playa de San Sebastián. At the eastern end of the promenade, just beyond the marina and around a headland, is the town's second, more secluded beach, Playa de la Cueva. Also sandy, it's less disturbed by harbour traffic and has great views across to Tenerife and Mount Teide.

Degollada de Peraza, La Laja and Roque Agando

9km/4hr hike. Bus #1 or #2 from San Sebastián, Mon–Sat 4 daily, 25min; or Valle Gran Rey, Mon–Sat 2 daily, 1hr 30min; bus #2 from Playa de Santiago, Mon–Sat 2 daily, 20min. Public buses, though infrequent, allow you to spend the day hiking in magnificent upland scenery. Ask the driver to drop you at Degollada de Peraza and you'll be at the spot that witnessed the 1488 murder of the island's

▲ SAN SEBASTIÁN MARINA

governor, now home to *Bar Peraza* (where drivers can leave their cars). From here, a 100-metre walk west along the road leads to a viewpoint; a further 100m along on the north side, there's a series of stone steps which climb onto a well-defined track. This track gradually widens, passing a lone house on a ridge before reaching a T-junction. Turn right onto what becomes an asphalt road, following it for five minutes or so to the Ermita de las Nieves, a tiny chapel surrounded by a huge plaza and viewing platform. Picnic tables make it an ideal spot for a break. Head round the church to follow a narrow track which climbs through stands of laurel trees before dropping down to the main road near Roque Agando. Continue 200m towards this huge rock, looking for a clearly signed turnoff to La Laja (3km) on the north side of the road. This steep, marked path drops through pine forest and groves of palms and orange trees to the scattered village of La Laja. From La Laja, San Sebastián is a pleasant but tiring 8km/3hr downhill hike away, following a lightly used minor road past a series of dams. A better alternative, though dependent on the bus services, is to continue the loop back to Degollada de Peraza, following the marked uphill path at a fork just above the village. If you're early or late for the bus, consider calling a taxi from *Bar Peraza*.

Playa de Santiago

Bus #2 from San Sebastián, Mon–Sat 2 daily, 40min. Ferries arrive to Valle Gran Rey, 3 daily, 20min; and San Sebastián, 3 daily, 25min. Though technically the second largest resort on the island, Playa de Santiago remains a small harbour town where only the presence of a few extra restaurants suggests tourism on any scale. Looming over it all, from a spectacular clifftop vantage point, is the gigantic five-star hotel *Jardín Tecina*. If you're not staying at the hotel, there's not much to do here, though you may be content to enjoy the island's sunniest weather on several large pebble beaches in a series of coves – some popular with nudists and hippies who sleep rough – that beckon just east of the *Tecina*. Most local hikes are dull by Gomeran standards, so the best excursion is to take a boat trip (€36) on the *Siron* to Los Organos – a series of organ-pipe shaped cliffs on the northeast side of the island – which leaves on Tuesdays, Thursdays and Sundays at 9am. Tickets can be purchased at *Bar Info* beyond the eastern end of Avenida Marítima.

Hotels

Garajonay

C/Ruiz de Padrón 17, San Sebastián ☎922 87 05 50, ⓕ922 87 05 50. Big, four-storey hotel in the centre of town, with 56 clean and simple, pine-furnished, en-suite rooms. The hotel usually has vacancies and also has some singles and triples. €42

Jardín Tecina

Playa de Santiago ☎922 14 58 50, ⓦwww.jardin-tecina.com. Luxurious self-contained resort with over four hundred rooms, five pools and restaurants, four bars and extensive sports facilities. Prices are for half-board. €142.

Parador Conde de la Gomera

Lomo de la Horca, San Sebastián ☎922 87 11 00, ⓦwww.parador.es. Graceful four-star Canarian-style mansion, high above town with breathtaking views. The hotel is consistently full and reservations should be made several weeks in advance. €116.

Torre del Conde

C/Ruíz de Padrón 19, San Sebastián ☎922 87 00 00, ⓕ922 87 13 14. Central hotel with simple elegant rooms – including some singles – all with TV and air-conditioning. Many also have balconies and there's a rooftop terrace equipped with sunloungers. Prices include breakfast; full- or half-board deals also available. €58.

Pensions

Casa Lolita

Laguna de Santiago, Playa de Santiago ☎922 89 55 50. The cheapest choice on the island – and blessed with fine views – has mattresses on the floor of the "student" rooms and windowless doubles (for married couples only) sharing a bathroom. €13.

Colombina

C/Ruiz de Padrón 83, San Sebastián ☎922 87 12 57. Reception open 7.30am–1pm & 4–7.30pm. Functional, clean and quiet property with friendly owners and a lovely roof-terrace. Rooms come with bath and there are some triples and good-value singles too. There's often room here when elsewhere is full. €36.

▼ PLAYA DE SANTIAGO

Colón

C/del Medio 59, San Sebastián ☎922 87 02 35. A collection of simple, clean and tastefully decorated rooms – though those with a balcony look out onto a noisy road and those without are windowless and dark. Some rooms have their own bathrooms and there are singles and triples available. If there's nobody in reception, ring at the green door for attention. €22.

La Gaviota

Avda. Maritima Playa de Santiago ☎922 89 51 35. Playa de Santiago's best pension, though more expensive than the rest. Some rooms are en suite and have a small balcony. Enquire at the restaurant below. €24.

Hespérides

C/Ruiz de Padrón 42, San Sebastián ☎922 87 13 05. Clean, basic, good-value pension right in the thick of things. Rooms have sinks but share bathrooms and there are some cheap singles beside a roof terrace, too. Ring at the door on the first floor for attention. €24.

Apartments

Canaris

C/Ruíz de Padrón 3, San Sebastián ☎922 14 14 53. Roomy, central and modern apartments, some with views over the Torre del Conde. Both the apartments and studios sleep two; the studios are particularly good value. €24.

Bellavista

C/Santa Ana, Playa de Santiago ☎922 89 55 70, ⊛www.casacanarias.co.uk. Complex of eleven attractive, English-run apartments of varying sizes – up to two bedrooms – all with sea views and some with balcony. €37.

Miramar

Orilla del Llano 3, San Sebastián ☎922 87 04 48. These smart, pine-furnished apartments are beyond the noise and bustle of the town centre. Units can sleep three and lets are for a minimum of three nights. If there's no answer, try *Bar Curva* next door. €36.

Negrin

Laguna de Santiago, Playa de Santiago ☎922 89 52 82. Modern and very basic apartments, sleeping up to three, with roof terraces offering good bay views. The apartments are in three separate blocks, of which Negrin 2 and 3 are quieter. €24.

Shops

Artesanía Santa Ana

C/del Medio 41, San Sebastián. Housed in a sixteenth-century former chapel, this is the largest of a series of tasteful souvenir shops along the Calle del Medio.

Cafés

Los Carabelas

Plaza de la Constitución, San Sebastián. Mon–Fri 7am–11pm. One of many cafés scattered in and around San Sebastián's two adjoining central plazas. This one is shaded by a couple of vast laurel trees, attracts an even mix of locals and visitors and has some of the best tapas around. Prices are moderate.

Restaurants

Breñusca

C/del Medio 11, San Sebastián. Closed Sun. Wood-furnished bar serving good, basic Canarian food – try the tasty stews such as *rancho canario* or the spicy rabbit in a garlicky *salmorejo* sauce. Open from 9am for breakfast.

La Casa Vieja

C/República de Chile 5, San Sebastián. Small simple bar where the TV blares football and you can choose inexpensive tapas from a chalkboard menu listing dishes such as octopus, rabbit and goat.

Cuatro Caminos

C/Ruiz de Padron 36, San Sebastián. Closed Sun. Tiny restaurant in a bar that's a popular local gathering place. The grilled fish is cheap and fresh.

Cubino

C/de la Virgen de Guadelupe 2, San Sebastián. Small, rustic and brightly lit bar and restaurant just off the main square serving inexpensive Canarian fare. Main courses include tuna steak and grilled chops. Order *papas arrugadas* to dip in the great home-made *mojo*.

La Cuevita

Avda. Marítima, Playa de Santiago. Closed Sun. Located in a candlelit natural cave, this restaurant has a massive selection of fish and meat including fine steaks and the good local fresh fish *vieja*. There's also a big and unusually imaginative dessert selection.

Marqués de Cristano

C/del Medio 24, San Sebastián ☏922 87 00 22. Classy and expensive restaurant in a restored eighteenth-century house. The great selection of tapas is served in a pleasant courtyard, while the restaurant above serves Canarian food with a decidedly gourmet twist.

El Paso

Avda. Marítima, Playa de Santiago. *El Paso* serves huge portions of beautifully cooked food making is justly popular with locals. Some spectacular photos show the 1999 storms, when the sea tore through the town.

Tagoror

Hotel Jardín Tecina, Playa de Santiago. With excellent views over the harbour and bay, *Tagoror* serves good tapas and has a large wine selection but otherwise its moderately expensive food – the usual fish, meat, paella and pizza – is nothing special.

La Tasca

C/Ruiz de Padrón 34, San Sebastián. Eve only. Multilingual menus indicate a mostly tourist clientele in this old, dimly lit Canarian house, where prices are reasonable and there are lots of fish and meat dishes plus a great mixed salad. Try the excellent spicy tomato soup to start.

Bars

Bar RP

Plaza de la Constitución, San Sebastián. Mon–Sat until 2am. One of the town's few nightlife spots, this is a sociable and hip bar with thirty-five varieties of beer available.

Clubs

Discomera

C/El Lamero 15, San Sebastián. Wed–Sat 11pm–3am. At the west end of the seafront promenade, this semi-outdoor club, playing chart music, only really gets busy on Fridays and Saturdays.

Valle Gran Rey

A deep gorge carved out of La Gomera's ancient rock, **Valle Gran Rey** contains a number of villages along its length and some low-key resorts where the valley reaches the ocean. In the late 1960s this area became the destination for German hippies, who have now been replaced by German students and professionals seeking an "alternative" beach holiday. Most of the upper valley is still terraced for agricultural use, but the comparatively large earnings from tourism have proved irresistible to locals who have built small apartment blocks for visitors near the coast. The three main villages, **Vueltas, La Calera** and **La Playa,** offer little more than the chance to relax on the sand-and-pebble beaches or in the pleasantly laid-back restaurants and bars. For something more active, sensational hiking is not far away.

▾ VUELTAS

Vueltas

The biggest and busiest of the three main villages in the valley, Vueltas is an untouristy place, where Canarians outnumber visitors and the few New-Agey shops and late-night bars do little to detract from the laid-back atmosphere. The beaches here are not terribly attractive however, so the chance to swim in the calm and generally clean waters of the town's harbour is very welcome.

Arrival and information

Buses #1 from San Sebastián (Mon–Sat 2–5 daily, 2hr 15min) stop in La Calera, Vueltas and La Playa. Ferries (3 daily) from Los Cristianos (1hr 20min), San Sebastián (35min) and Playa de Santiago (20min) dock at Vueltas. The valley's **tourist office** (Mon–Sat 9am–1.30pm; ☏922/805458) is in La Playa, on the road that runs parallel to the promenade.

Boat trips

Boat trips to the impressive cliff face of Los Organos, with its high wall of six-sided basalt columns, depart daily – except in rough weather – from Vueltas harbour. The standard six-and-a-half-hour trip is done by the *Siron* (☎922/805 480; Tues–Sun 10.30am; €30) and the *Tina* (☎922/805 699; daily 10.30am; €30), and also includes a stop so passengers can have a swim off a small beach only accessible by sea. Food is provided and you may also see dolphins and whales. For specifically whale-watching jaunts, tailor-made yachting, deep-sea fishing trips and visits to Hierro and La Palma, enquire at the Bait and Tackle shop (closed Sun) just inland of the plaza in Vueltas.

Argaga tropicfruitgarden

☎922 69 70 04. Tues & Fri: April–Sept 10am–5pm; Oct–March 11am–4pm. €9. The tropical orchard **Argaga tropicfruitgarden** is a fifteen-minute walk south of Vueltas – following first the cliffs opposite the harbour and then a track a short way up the Barranco Argaga (past the "private" signs). Originally developed by enthusiasts as an organic garden for fruits and flowers, visitor interest has led to the orchard being opened for frequent, pleasantly informal tours (in English on request). These concentrate on sampling around a dozen of the exotic fruits grown here, accompanied by salient information on their cultivation.

Barranco Argaga hike

Beyond the Argaga tropicfruitgarden the steep and narrow Barranco Argaga gorge is an amazing sight and offers great hiking. For the energetic, there's a strenuous but excellent loop from Valle Gran Rey, along which the interesting terrain and great views make it one of the island's premier hikes. A marked, but unsignposted, path clambers steeply up Barranco Argaga to the hamlet of Gerián. From here, fork left onto an unmarked but obvious water-channel path to the chapel Ermita de Nuestra Señora de Guadalupe, high on the south slope of the gorge. The path continues from the chapel, dropping gradually into the ravine bed – ignore a marked path on the right to Chipude. Once at the base of the ravine the route climbs again and continues straight over the ridge ahead – ignore turn-offs to the right and left along the ridge – then descends steeply into Valle Gran Rey. Turn left along the path at the valley bottom, follwing a dry stream bed back to La Calera.

▼ SUNSET DRUMMING

LA PLAYA

Fisch & Co
La Rueda
(Car rental)
El Fotógrafo

LA CALERA

Centro de Salud
(Medical Centre)

Pharmacy

Bank

Servicos Integrados

Playa
del Inglés

Pharmacy **VUELTAS**

Chaico del
Conde

Alafi Rentals
(Bike rental)

Playa
Vueltas

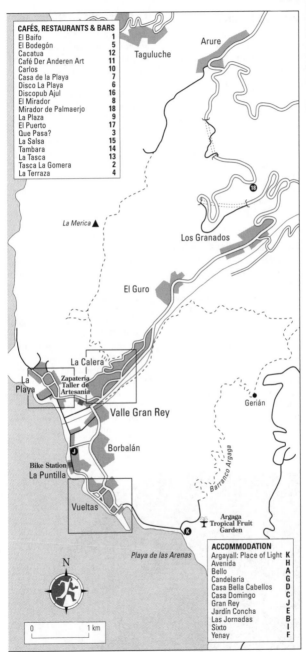

CAFÉS, RESTAURANTS & BARS

El Baifo	1
El Bodegón	5
Cacatua	12
Café Der Anderen Art	11
Carlos	10
Casa de la Playa	7
Disco La Playa	6
Discopub Ajul	16
El Mirador	8
Mirador de Palmaerjo	18
La Plaza	9
El Puerto	17
Que Pasa?	3
La Salsa	15
Tambara	14
La Tasca	13
Tasca La Gomera	2
La Terraza	4

Taguluche

Arure

La Merica ▲

Los Granados

El Guro

La Calera

Zapatería Taller de Artesanía

La Playa

Valle Gran Rey

Gerián

Borbalán

Bike Station
La Puntilla

Barranco Argaga

Vueltas

Argaga Tropical Fruit Garden

Playa de las Arenas

N

0	1 km

ACCOMMODATION

Argayall: Place of Light	K
Avenida	H
Bello	A
Candelaria	G
Casa Bella Cabellos	D
Casa Domingo	C
Gran Rey	J
Jardín Concha	E
Las Jornadas	B
Sixto	I
Yenay	F

Playa de las Arenas

Playa de las Arenas refers to a series of coves, southeast along the coast from Valle Gran Rey's main settlements. Home to a collection of hippies who call it Rainbow Beach and have painted a rainbow on the rock at its entrance, local expatriate Germans prefer to know it as *Schweinebucht* (bay of pigs), neatly expressing their feelings about its residents. The beaches are popular with nudists. To get here, follow the coast south of Vueltas and be prepared for some scrambling over loose tracks and rock faces.

La Playa and Playa del Inglés

A collection of modern buildings, clustered around a beach and short promenade, La Playa has an easy-going seaside atmosphere. It's well-positioned to take advantage of Valle Gran Rey's best beaches, the most crowded of which is the sand-and-pebble strand that stretches out in front of the resort. From La Playa, a dirt track – the only one leading north out of the village – leads to the most popular nudist beach, Playa del Inglés.

La Calera and La Merica hikes

Two hikes: 3–4hr. At the point where the mouth of the valley opens out into the delta, a cluster of houses have clawed their way up a cliff to form La Calera, the quietest of the three main villages in the valley. Steep steps and winding alleys connect the old buildings enjoying great valley and sea views in this,. Above it the magnificent peak La Merica offers strenuous hiking on rocky trails with tremendous views. A well-trodden track starts from the high road at the up-valley end of La Calera, marked by a large wooden sign. After winding up treeless, volcanic cliffs, the path branches off to a viewpoint near the top – marked by a windsock – with La Playa almost vertically below and an inaccessible collection of steep gorges to the north. This hike can also form part of an excellent half-day hike from Arure at the head of the valley. By taking the bus (or hitching) up to this village, you can head east along an unsigned but obvious dirt road that later becomes a rough track following the stunning ridge south, via the summit of La Merica and the viewpoint

▾ RAINBOW BEACH

described above before finally dropping back down to La Calera.

Hotels

Argayall: Place of Light

Playa de Las Arenas ☎922 69 70 08, ⊛www.argayall.com. New Age centre, 15min walk from Vueltas in an isolated spot by the beach. Both singles and doubles are available and prices include vegetarian full board. A broad activity programme includes meditation, reiki, yoga, African dance and drumming.. Reception is open 10am–1pm, but closed Tues. €84.

Gran Rey

La Puntilla ☎922 80 58 59, ⊛www.hotel-granrey.com. This large waterfront hotel is the valley's most luxurious accommodation. Facilities include tennis courts, a pool and a large roof terrace, while the en-suite rooms have air-conditioning and TVs. Some singles available. Prices include breakfast. €114.

Pensions

Candelaria

Vueltas ☎922 80 54 02. Simple, very popular pension with a large sundeck and good sea views from the roof, on one of the backstreets of the old port. There are rooms of various sizes, styles and prices – plus some basic apartments (from €25 per night for two) – some with private bathrooms. €20.

Casa Bella Cabellos

Calera ☎922 80 51 82. Restored old Canarian home with wooden balconies, surrounded by lush vegetation. Run by an amenable old lady, this place has simple doubles, a studio and a four-bed apartment. The house is a bit off the beaten track on the old village road. €30.

Jardín Concha

La Calera ☎922 80 60 63. Elegant, hotel-quality lodgings in the first place in the valley to rent rooms to foreigners. Views from the patios are superb. The pension runs a couple of functional apartments nearby. En-suite doubles €27.

Las Jornadas

La Playa ☎922 80 50 47, ⊜casa-maria@terra.es. Excellently positioned in front of the beach, above a large restaurant (see p.155), the highlight of this pension is the roof terrace overlooking the sea, while the simple rooms (some tiny) share grubby bathrooms. €20.

Apartments

Avenida

Vueltas ☎922 80 54 61. Four-storey apartment block in a splendid waterfront location, with sea views from all balconies. Units are equipped with kitchenettes and sleep two. €20.

Bello

La Playa ☎922 80 51 15. Spacious, well-equipped, modern apartments with balconies, beside the promenade. All sleep two, and while some overlook the beach, others face the wall of an apartment block and are thus darker but less expensive. Enquire at Bar Yaya below. €30.

Casa Domingo

La Playa ☎ & ⊕922 80 51 31. Bright, clean, pine-furnished apartments, sleeping two to four people, close to the beach in a four-storey house surrounded by banana groves. €30.

Sixto

Vueltas ☎922 80 53 32. Well-worn but good-value apartments in the centre of Vueltas, run by a friendly elderly Canarian who often comes down to the quay to meet arriving boats. Apartments are spacious, sleep up to three and share a small roof terrace. €22.

▼ LA CALERA

Yenay

Vueltas ☎922 80 54 71. Large basic block with standard apartments, studios and a couple of basic windowless rooms. The roof terrace has great views. €20.

Shops

El Fotógrafo

La Playa ☎922 805 654. The best source of original postcards in La Gomera. The shop is also useful for hiking maps and guides (most in German) and has a photo processing service.

Zapatería Taller de Artesanía

By the road between La Calera and La Playa. Old-fashioned cobblers where shoes are made to measure (around €50), repaired or widened. Off-the-peg handmade shoes are also available, as are other leather goods.

Cafés

Café Der Anderen Art

Vueltas. Daily except Thurs 10am–1pm & 5pm–midnight. Small trendy café in the centre of town, serving good continental breakfasts, plus cakes and crêpes all day.

Carlos

La Calera. Mon–Sat 9am–7pm. Carlos's tiny outside terrace overflows with people watching the valley's busiest road while they sample the ice cream and freshly pressed fruit juices.

Casa de la Playa

La Playa. Mon–Sat 10am–10pm. Consistently busy, large, shady terrace beside a banana plantation on the edge of La Playa – the place to hang out at sunset. Serves good snacks and *bocadillos* along with ice cream, shakes and juices.

Tambara

Vueltas. Open 5pm–1am; closed Wed. Small café-bar with great views over the sea. Spots on the tiny terrace are hard to come by but the interior, decorated with Turkish mosaics, is almost as nice. The tapas are better value than the overpriced sandwiches and cocktails.

Restaurants

El Baifo

La Playa ☏922/805 775. Closed Fri & July. Excellent, moderately expensive Malaysian restaurant that makes the most of local fresh fish to offer an alternative to the usual Gomeran cuisine. Vegetarians are well catered for.

El Mirador

La Calera. Closed Thurs. Large moderately priced restaurant with great valley views that's a good place to start or finish the day. Breakfasts include *bocadillos* and fresh juices, the tapas and salads make for a good light lunch, and dinner sees the usual fish and meat options, served with *papas arrugadas* and excellent home-made *mojo*.

La Plaza

La Calera. Closed Thurs. Basic, unexciting bar on the main road by the taxi rank, popular thanks

to its low prices and large portions of food like rabbit and chicken *en salsa*.

El Puerto

Vueltas. Closed Wed. Harbour-side restaurant that is a favourite with locals. Food is suitably basic – the €6.50 menu of the day typically including salad, a tuna steak and ice cream. The grilled fish platter (€15) for two people is the restaurant's speciality.

La Salsa

Vueltas ☏922 80 55 18. Nov–April 6–11.30pm, closed Wed. Bright and trendy restaurant with bold colour schemes and great vegetarian food. The varied menu includes tacos, Thai curry and tofu dishes. Though a bit pricey by local standards, the big portions are worth it.

La Terraza

La Playa. Closed Mon. Large enclosed terrace visited exclusively by holidaymakers, this place specializes in big, good-value portions of large pork chops with *papas arrugadas*, pizzas and paella.

Las Jornadas

La Playa. Closed Tues. Popular restaurant on the beachfront, below the pension of the same name. Large portions of home-made food include a massive Spanish omelette, a tasty paella and a superb grilled chicken breast (each around €6–8). Check the blackboard for the fresh dishes of the day.

Mirador de Palmaerjo

Head of the valley ☏922 80 58 68. Open Tues–Sat. Designed by Canarian artist César Manrique, this restaurant-cum-viewpoint provides dizzying views of Valle

▲ THE PROMENADE, LA PLAYA

Gran Rey. The relatively expensive gourmet variations on old Canarian favourites are worth a stop on the way back from hiking in the uplands, but only if you have access to a car or taxi. Book ahead to get the best views.

Bars

Bar La Tasca

Vueltas. A tropical atmosphere permeates this bar, with the best cocktails in the valley and board games on each table. Empty before 10pm.

Bar Que Pasa?

La Playa. Laid-back friendly hangout with ethnic decor, good tapas, fine cocktails and a large library of books.

El Bodegón

La Playa. Closed Sun. Though chiefly a mediocre restaurant, this place is also popular with local men who occasionally gather here to play melancholy Gomeran folk music – and some salsa too. Performances are ad hoc, so keep an eye out or ask if anything's planned.

Cacatua

Vueltas. Closed Mon. Easily the most popular cocktail bar in the valley, with several spacious rooms, a big patio and a lively vibe. It tends to get going a little later than elsewhere.

Tasca La Gomera

La Playa. Well-run pub with pleasant tiny outdoor terrace and occasional live music.

Clubs

Discopub Ajul

Vueltas. Tues–Sun 10.30pm–4.30am. €3. Nondescript disco that livens up at the weekend and on Thursdays when the hippies from Playa de Las Arenas get their drums out and add even more colour to the mix of chart, trance, salsa and reggae played here.

Disco La Playa

La Playa. Wed–Sun 10pm–5am. Free. La Playa's late night venue can be fun at the weekends or if there's live music. On other nights the scene can be a bit desperate, though, and don't arrive before 1am or you're likely to have the place to yourself.

Northern La Gomera

Atlantic trade winds regularly bring clouds and misty rain to **northern La Gomera**, making its damp, lush valleys the island's most fertile. Bananas grow here in large quantities, particularly around Hermigua, and much of the tiny population on this side of the island is involved in agriculture. At the head of these valleys lies one of the world's most ancient forests and La Gomera's most outstanding attraction, the **Parque Nacional de Garajonay**. Apart from a mass of moss-cloaked laurel trees, this UNESCO World Heritage site contains around four hundred species of flora and is one of the last vestiges of an ecosystem that was once widespread around the Mediterranean. With few specific attractions and unreliable weather, visitors don't tend to base themselves in this part of the island – which is a pity as the area is highly rewarding, particularly for hikers, who can enjoy the eerie atmosphere of the park's overgrown trails and the wild and picturesque coast.

Garajonay hike

5km/2hr return hike. Bus to Pajarito: Linea 1 from San Sebastián, Mon–Sat 4–5 daily, 30min; or Valle Gran Rey, Mon–Sat 2 daily, 1hr 30min. The most obvious excursion in the national park is the hike to its highest point, which offers superb views over the dense tree canopy and beyond to neighbouring islands – weather permitting. To climb the peak, head up from Pajarito, the road junction where the bus stops, from where the route is signposted "Alto de Garajonay 2.5". The path climbs steeply, through the laurel forest until eventually the trees thin and you arrive at a T-junction on a ridge and a signpost to "Alto de Garajonay" and "Contadero". Turn left for the Alto and you soon arrive at the summit where in good weather there are views of the islands of El Hierro and La Palma. From the summit simply retrace your steps back to Pajarito.

▼ LAUREL FOREST

The legend of Garajonay

The mountain Garajonay is named for Gomera's answer to Romeo and Juliet, **Gara** and **Jonay**, a Gomeran princess and a humble peasant boy from Tenerife who visited his princess by paddling over on inflated goatskins – or so the Guanche legend goes. Neither family were keen on the couple's relationship but their love ran far deeper than their differences in status, and so, determined never to be parted, they clambered to the top of Garajonay and ran each other through with lances of laurel wood, choosing death rather than separation and naming the mountain in the process.

Alto de Contadero to Hermigua hike

9km/4hr hike one-way. Bus to Pajarito: Linea 1 from San Sebastián, Mon–Sat 2 daily, 30min; or Valle Gran Rey, Mon–Sat 2 daily, 1hr 30min. This scenically spectacular and wonderfully varied hike is easily the best in La Gomera, and made even more attractive by being almost entirely downhill. It's a one-way hike, so you have to rely on using the island's bus services to complete a round-trip from San Sebastián, or get a taxi back to your base.

The first part of the hike follows the route above to Alto de Garajonay as far as the T-junction where you turn right for Contadero. From here it's around 1km descending to a wide dirt track. A right turn here soon brings you to the main road and the lay-by Alto de Contadero. Follow the trail signposted "El Cedro 4.8" which drops through overgrown ancient forests along one of the most magical sections of this walk. Around 3km down this trail you come to a fork where you should follow signs to "Arroyo de El Cedro". The track crosses La Gomera's only stream (arroyo) several times on the way to a parking area on a dirt road. The *Mudéjar*-style chapel Ermita de Nuestra Señora de Lourdes is a short way beyond this on paths marked "Caserío de El Cedro".

Continuing on to El Cedro you arrive at a dirt road on the edge of the hamlet. Turn right here and then left at a T-junction, following signs to *Bar La Vista*. The dirt road snakes its way to the bottom of the valley before arriving at a small ford. Just to the right is the location of El Cedro's water tunnel, while the main path carries on across the ford and to the right, following the stream.

The hamlet is soon left behind as the distinct path passes a small waterfall, before spectacular views open up of the Hermigua Valley. Descending steeply the path is clear as you pass a couple of dams and an old *gofio* mill – the grindstone is still there.

Further down the valley, as you pass banana plantations, follow a pipeline which you leave only at some short steep steps to a minor sealed road. Turn right here and follow the road to some stairs that come just before a sharp bend in the road, where benches are set into a concrete road-barrier. Descend the steps here to a plaza where buses will stop if you flag them down or there's a phone to call a local taxi (☎922 88 00 47 or 922 88 00 09).

El Cedro

Set amid lush cultivated terraces and dense laurel thickets, El Cedro is the national park at its

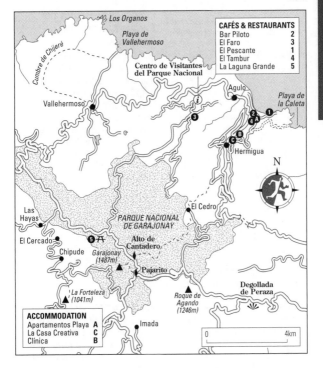

CAFÉS & RESTAURANTS
Bar Piloto	2
El Faro	3
El Pescante	1
El Tambur	4
La Laguna Grande	5

ACCOMMODATION
Apartamentos Playa	A
La Casa Creativa	C
Clínica	B

best. This modest hamlet makes a good place to stop on longer hikes or, as the only place to stay in the park, a destination in itself. Other than the spectacular surrounding scenery, El Cedro is also known for an exciting short hike through a claustrophobic 575m underground water tunnel – allow an hour, bring a torch and expect wet feet. The tunnel took 26 years to chisel by hand and was used to help irrigate Hermigua's thirsty banana plantations.

Hermigua

Linea 3 from San Sebastián, Mon–Sat 2 daily, 25min; or Vallehermoso, Mon–Sat 2 daily, 45min. Scattered the length of a pretty ravine, and fed by water from La Gomera's only stream, the small town of Hermigua is in the island's lushest valley. The presence of a relatively plentiful supply of water here has encouraged prolific banana cultivation for over a century. The town broadly divides into an upper and lower village. The former, Valle Alto, is marked by the sixteenth-century Iglesia de Santo Domingo (rarely open) beside a convent of the same name. The lower village, Valle Bajo, has at its centre a small plaza beside the modern Nuestra Señora de la Emancipación church. Another collection of buildings is further down the valley by the large pebble beach, but huge Atlantic rollers and strong undercurrents mean that the only spot to swim here is the large sea-water pool.

Playa de la Caleta

The quiet black sand-and-pebble La Caleta beach (6km/1hr east of Hermigua) is generally a safe option for a swim. A little restaurant, open on fair-weather days between April and October, serves fish caught by fishermen living in a couple of nearby huts. The dirt road to Playa de la Caleta begins near the plaza in Valle Bajo and heads east up a steep road to the top of a headland, from where it descends into a valley before arriving at the beach.

Agulo

Linea 3 from San Sebastián, Mon–Sat 2 daily, 30min; or Vallehermoso, Mon–Sat 2 daily, 40min. Huddled on a tight shelf above the sea and below some mighty cliffs, the charming seventeenth-century village of Agulo holds a maze of cobbled alleys and whitewashed houses making it well worth a quick visit. If you arrive by car, it's better to park on the main road rather than try to negotiate the narrow streets.

▼ AGULO

Centro de Visitantes del Parque Nacional de Garajonay

☎992 80 09 93. Tues–Sun 9.30am–4.30pm. Free. Bus Linea 3 from San Sebastián, Mon–Sat 2–4 daily, 35min; or Vallehermoso, Mon–Sat 3–5 daily, 35min. Located well outside the national park, the visitor centre is near Agulo, a two-kilometre uphill hike from *Las Rosas* restaurant bus stop on the main road. The centre has a few displays on the park, a supply of books and maps (there's a wider range in San Sebastián and Valle Gran Rey) and a diverting little museum of folk history with a reconstructed traditional Gomeran home. Ask the staff about their free weekly English guided hikes.

Vallehermoso

Linea 3 from San Sebastián, Mon–Sat 2 daily, 1hr 10min. The setting of Vallehermoso, "beautiful valley", is undoubtedly picturesque. The town nestles between steep ridges, and below the towering volcanic monolith Roque Cano. Focal point is the Plaza de la Constitución, a small plaza

▲ VALLEHERMOSO

surrounded by bars, shops, banks (with ATMs), a post office, a medical centre and a petrol station. Heading north from here, it's a thirty-minute walk to the sea. The tempestuous surf generally rules out bathing, but work on a large bathing pool is underway.

Cumbre de Chijeré hike

10km/4hr hike. To get an appreciation of the beauty of the valley and magnitude of the cliffs on this side of the coast, one of the best hikes is the excellent loop along the Cumbre de Chijeré. From Vallehermoso head north towards the sea, leaving the road to ascend a steep-sided gorge a few hundred metres shy of the beach. Weaving between three houses, the trail – soon marked by blue arrows and red dots – zigzags its way up the rocky arid slopes, with views of rugged cliffs and Teide on Tenerife in the distance. As the path reaches the top of the Cumbre de Chijeré ridge, a landscape of ochre rock eroded into swirling shapes is revealed. A dirt road, which leads as far as the viewpoint on the tip of

the ridge nearby, runs inland past a tiny chapel. Once past the chapel, follow a narrow track off to the right, through woods with more great views over the cliffs to the west. The path rejoins the main track at another chapel, where a short way further on another narrow path turns off to the (left) east, snaking its way through dense Laurasilva forest, then descending through terraces, back into the centre of Vallehermoso.

▼ CUMBRE DE CHIJERÉ

Chipude

Linea 1 from San Sebastián, Mon–Sat 2 daily, 1hr; or Valle Gran Rey, Mon–Sat 2 daily, 45min. Until two hundred years ago Chipude was La Gomera's largest town, but there's little trace of this former grandeur today. Only the sixteenth-century Moorish **Iglesia de la Virgen de la Candelaria**, dominating the central plaza, hints at the former importance of the town. Otherwise there are a couple of bars offering basic food and accommodation, making the town the most readily accessible base in the uplands.

La Fortaleza

4km/2hr hike. Bus to Chipude; see above. Once a place of considerable spiritual significance to the Guanches, and still the most impressive landmark in the uplands, **La Fortaleza** mesa makes a superb two hour round-trip from Chipude. Starting out along the road south to La Dama, the track up the hill to the left of the road is obvious. As the trail ascends the final section to the summit plateau it becomes less clear and it's a case of making your own route over bare rock – a head for heights is essential. The top of the hill is almost uniformly flat and blustery winds are common, but excellent views over Chipude, the national park and El Hierro island compensate. For Guanches, this was an important place of retreat and worship and remains of stone circles have been found here, along with bone fragments, suggesting sacrifices.

Pensions

Amaya

Vallehermoso ☎922 80 00 73. Bar and pension with basic single and double rooms sharing bathrooms, or more luxurious options with private bath, TV and fridge. €20.

Bar La Vista

El Cedro ☎922 88 09 49. Offers simple rooms and runs a small campsite (€2 per site) – the island's only one, and the only place you can legally pitch in the park. €24.

Casa Bernardo

C/Triana 4, Vallehermoso ☎922 80 08 49. Excellent value pension whose friendly, relaxed owners speak English and offer clean and simple singles and doubles, along with use of a communal kitchen. Two apartments (€28) on the roof are also good options, but require a three-night minimum stay. €20.

Clínica

Carretera General 72, Hermigua ☎ & ☎922 88 10 40. Five rooms are offered in this former clinic turned pension. It's a sociable

▼ LA FORTALEZA

place and well set up for groups (up to eight people) with a communal kitchen, eating area and pleasant little garden. Single rooms available. €20–25.

Pensión Sonia

Chipude ☎922 80 41 58. Bar on the church plaza with modern and scrupulously clean, hotel-quality, en-suite rooms. €22.

Apartments

Apartamentos Playa

Hermigua ☎922 88 07 58. Clean basic apartments sleeping two and overlooking the shingle beach. Run by the neighbouring bar *Los Prismas*. €24.

La Casa Creativa

Carretera General 58, Hermigua ☎922 88 10 23. Well-equipped, German-run apartments, sharing a pleasant terrace and small pool, with the option of full-board deals at a wholefood restaurant (see p.164). €41.

Shops

Artesanía

Plaza de la Constitución, Vallehermoso. Mon–Fri & Sun 8.30am–1pm & 5–8pm; Sat 8.30am–1pm only. Small shop beside *Bar Central* selling lots of local produce at reasonable prices. The Gomeran goat's cheese (*queso del país*) is particularly recommended. There are also musical instruments, cigars and spirits.

Centro de Visitantes del Parque Nacional de Garajonay

☎992 80 09 93. Tues–Sun 9.30am–4.30pm. The centre's craft workshops produce and sell pottery, musical instruments

– tambourines and castanets – and baskets.

Alfarería Tradicional

El Cercado. Daily 9am–2pm & 4–7pm. The small village of El Cercado is home to several pottery shops and workshops specializing in *Alfarería* – a traditional technique in which pots are made without a wheel and rubbed with red earth before glazing.

Los Telares

C/General del Norte, Hermigua. Daily 9am–6pm. Weaving studio in a renovated house where rugs are the speciality among all manner of reasonably priced crafts and souvenirs.

Cafés

Amaya

Plaza de la Constitución, Vallehermoso. Overlooking the plaza, this consistently busy café-cum-bar serves coffees, basic food and tapas.

El Pescante

Hermigua. June–September noon–late. Beside the beach and the sea-water pool, this place offers a small menu of tapas and fish dishes. In the evenings an eclectic mix of recorded music is played to young Hermiguans and a handful of holidaymakers.

Restaurants

Agana

Avda. Guillermo Ascancio 5, Vallehermoso. Wed–Mon 10am–11pm. This combined bar and restaurant is one of few eating options in Vallehehermoso and serves a range of simple, inexpensive traditional meat and fish dishes.

La Laguna Grande

La Laguna Grande. Tues–Sun 9am–6pm. In a large former crater that's now a popular picnic spot, this restaurant serves good, moderately priced stews and some excellent *mojo* and is often busy with day trippers from Tenerife.

La Montaña

Las Hayas. Sun–Fri 8am–8pm. Serving superb, reasonably priced vegetarian cuisine, this bar puts the uneventful hamlet of Las Hayas on the map. It specializes in stews made from home-grown and picked-to-order ingredients. The almond cake drizzled in palm honey is a delicious and typically Gomeran way to finish the meal.

La Casa Creativa

Carretera General 58, Hermigua ☎922 88 10 23. Daily 9am–11pm. Moderately expensive restaurant that creatively and successfully blends German wholefood fare with traditional Gomeran cuisine.

El Faro

Hermigua. Noon–4pm & 7–10pm. Closed Wed & June. At the sea end of town above *Bar Piloto*, this place serves substantial but moderately priced meals including a great fish paella (pre-order in the morning) and meat dishes such as lamb with *papas arrugadas*.

Bar Piloto

Hermigua. Closed Sun. Inexpensive bar food served to three small tables that look out to sea. The menu changes daily, but often includes fresh tuna and a good home-made *mojo*. The Canarian potatoes with sesame and palm honey is a unique local spin on an old favourite.

Sonia

Chipude ☎922 80 41 58. No-frills bar with inexpensive, basic Gomeran food – large dishes of *gofio* stand on tables ready to accompany the menu that's limited to one daily soup and main course.

El Tambor

Centro de Visitantes. Tues–Sun 9.30am–4.30pm. Simple, rustic and inexpensive restaurant with great views from a small patio and excellent simple Gomeran food.

La Vista

El Cedro ☎922 88 09 49. In the centre of El Cedro hamlet, this bar has picturesque views over the Hermigua Valley and hearty, inexpensive Gomeran food.

▼ EL TAMBOR

RTE. TAMBOR
POTAJE DE BERROS
ALMOGROTE
QUESO DE CABRA
JAMON SERRANO
ENSALADA MIXTA
GARBANZAS
PAPAS RELLENAS
CHAMPIÑONES AL AJILLO
CROQUETAS DE PESCADO
ATUN EN MOJO HERVIDO
CALAMARES A LA ROMANA
POLLO ASADO
ESTOFADO DE TERNERA
CARNE DE CABRA
LECHE ASADA - TARTA - HELADOS

Essentials

Essentials

Arrival

The majority of international flights to Tenerife land at **Tenerife South Airport** (Reina Sofía), near El Médano, with **Tenerife North** (Los Rodeos), near La Laguna and Santa Cruz, handling largely domestic traffic. **La Gomera's airport** receives no international flights, and with exorbitant prices for domestic connections, the most ecomanical option is to fly to Tenerife and take a ferry from Los Cristianos to San Sebastián.

Tenerife

The majority of holidaymakers have a free transfer to their hotel included in their package. For those travelling independently, taxis and frequent public buses run from each airport to major local towns.

Tenerife South (Reina Sofía)

☎922 75 90 00, ⌐www.aena.es. Bus #341 to Santa Cruz, 23 daily, 50min; #340 to Puerto de la Cruz, 4 daily, 1hr 25min; #487 to Playa de Las Américas and Los Cristianos 15 daily, 45min. Approximate taxi fares: Santa Cruz €48; Puerto de la Cruz €70; Las Américas €16.

Tenerife North (Los Rodeos)

☎922 63 56 35, ⌐www.aena.es. Bus #107, 108 & 109 to Santa Cruz, 27–30 daily, 30min; #340 to Puerto de la Cruz, 4 daily, 45min. Approximate taxi fares: Santa Cruz €20; Puerto de la Cruz €40; Las Américas €58.

La Gomera

Three companies make the trip from Los Cristianos to La Gomera. The Benchijingua Express (☎922 62 82 31, ⌐www .fredolsen.es; 5 daily, 45min; €39 return) and Isla de la Gomera (☎902 45 46 45, ⌐www.trasmediterranea.es; 2–3 daily, 90min; €26 return) head solely to San Sebastián. The third company is the Garajonay Exprés catamaran (☎902 34 34 50, ⌐www.garajonayexpres.com; 3 daily), running to San Sebastián (45min; €29 return), Playa Santiago (1hr; €34 return) and Valle Gran Rey (1hr 20min; €36 return). You can also make short hops between these Gomeran towns for €2–4.

Information

The **Spanish National Tourist Office** (SNTO) produces a number of maps and pamphlets on the Canaries. Most of what they have can be picked up at tourist offices on Tenerife and La Gomera (see the box at the beginning of each Places chapter for location details), along with a number of local maps, leaflets and accommodation listings unavailable elsewhere. The main and best-stocked offices are at Reina Sofía airport and in Santa Cruz on Tenerife and San Sebastián on La Gomera.

European **newspapers** reach Tenerife within a day of publication. A big ex-pat presence means that local news and tourist-oriented listings fill the many free English-language newspapers. Ones to look out for are *Island Connections* (⌐www.ic-web.com), *Tenerife News* (⌐www.tennews.com), *The Western Sun*, *The Weekly Canarian* and *Here and Now*.

On the **Web**, official sites for the islands – ⌐www.webtenerife.com and ⌐www .gomera-island.com – are worth browsing for a glossy overview. Of the many commercial websites, most are preoccupied with selling package holidays, but ⌐www.etenerife.com stands out as one of the more informative options. Another decent site is ⌐www.tizz.com/spain/ which has links to a Canarian section – though mainly in Spanish. Finally, for an entertaining forum with opinions of other holiday makers go to ⌐www.holidays-uncovered.co.uk.

Transport

Getting around **Tenerife** is straightforward. An excellent island-wide bus service is supplemented by plentiful and fairly cheap taxis. But for added flexibility, and getting off the beaten track, renting a car or a bicycle is practical and inexpensive. Getting around **La Gomera** is more difficult: the bus network is skeletal, making renting a car almost essential. If you want someone else to do the driving, a good selection of bus **tours** are widely advertised in hotels and travel agents in the main resorts.

Buses

Local **buses** (generally referred to as *guagua*) offer an inexpensive service all over **Tenerife**. Fares are low – Los Cristianos to Reina Sofía Airport, for example, costs €3 – and can be made around a third cheaper by purchasing a Bono-Bus card, a pre-paid ticket available on Tenerife only which is fed into a machine on the bus and, once you've told the driver your destination, has the fare deducted. The cards (from €12) can be bought from newsagents and news-stands.

Timetables are generally attached to main bus stops, which are marked with either the destination of the bus (*destino*) or its origin (*desede*). Most routes stop in the early evening and some don't run on Saturdays. The principal island routes are shown on the cover flap at the front of this book, but if you plan to use the network extensively, pick up the excellent map and timetable available from major bus stations, some kiosks and most tourist information centres. Alternatively, call the 24-hour information service – in both English and Spanish – ☎922 53 13 00, or check ⓦwww.titsa.com.

La Gomera is served by three public **bus services**, which leave from the ferry terminal in San Sebastián with a stop at the town's bus station on Via de Ronda. Though infrequent, they do offer non-drivers a way to access some of the island's best hikes. Linea #1 heads up to Valle Gran Rey via Chipude (2 daily, 1hr 40min, €4); Linea #2 runs to Playa de Santiago (2–4 daily, 1hr 10min, €4), and Linea #3 goes to Vallehermoso via Hermigua (2 daily, 1hr 30min, €3.50).

Taxis

Taxis in the islands' major towns and resorts are generally easy to find. The minimum charge is €2, with surcharges added for luggage, travel between 10pm and 6am or on Sundays, and journeys to the airports or docks. Fares also vary according to traffic conditions – make sure the driver uses the meter – but expect to pay €15 from Los Cristianos or Playa de Las Américas to Reina Sofía Airport, and €54 from Puerto de la Cruz.

Taxis can be particularly useful to shuttle you to or from hikes and fares are reasonable if there are several of you to split the cost.

Taxi companies

Santa Cruz ☎922 21 00 59 or at the main rank in Plaza de España.

Puerto de la Cruz ☎922 38 49 10 or at the main rank beside Plaza del Charco.

Las Américas ☎922 79 14 07 or from the ranks on the main seafront road.

Los Cristianos ☎922 79 03 52 or from beside the Plaza del Carmen.

Las Galletas ☎922 39 09 24.

San Sebastián ☎922 87 05 24 or at the harbour beside Plaza de las Américas.

Cars

Car rental on Tenerife is inexpensive and practical for exploring areas – including the national park – that are poorly served by the bus network. Rural roads are often steep, twisting and tiring to drive, but they are at least relatively quiet – in the towns, particularly Santa Cruz, driving can be a hectic experience and finding a parking space is often a problem.

To rent a car you need to be over 21 (though some operators won't rent to anyone under 25) and have had your licence for over a year. EU licences (either pink or pink and green) are accepted as are most other foreign licences, though the latter officially need to be accompanied by an International Driving Permit. Most operators also require a €30 deposit or a credit-card number and sometimes an island address as well.

Rates start at around €20 per day for a small hatchback, and all operators offer substantial discounts for rentals of a week or more. You can also save money by using smaller local operators, though be sure to check the car's condition. If using international companies, book in advance for discounted rates that may be enabled by membership of an automobile club like the AA. In addition, if booking a holiday through a travel agent, consider a fly-drive deal. Rental usually includes tax, unlimited mileage and full insurance (including collision damage waiver), but these details should be double-checked with any operator – particularly smaller ones who sometimes build odd exclusions into contracts. Most operators will not allow you to island hop with their car and don't include petrol in prices – lead-free petrol (*sin plomo*) costs around €0.60 per litre.

Car rental companies

Auto Reisen Central reservations ☏922 39 22 55, Tenerife South Airport ☏922 39 22 16; ☏www.autoreisen.es.

Autos El Carmen Valle Gran Rey ☏922 80 50 29.

Avis Tenerife South Airport ☏922 39 20 56, Tenerife North Airport ☏922 25 87 13, Los Cristianos ☏922 75 35 44, El Duque ☏922 71 44 14, Playa de las Américas ☏922 79 10 01, Puerto de la Cruz ☏922 38 46 98, Santa Cruz ☏922 24 12 94, La Puntilla Valle Gran Rey ☏922 80 55 27; ☏www.avis.com.

Cicar Tenerife North ☏922 63 26 42, Tenerife South ☏922 63 26 42, Santa Cruz ☏922 29 24 25; ☏www.cicar.com.

Hertz Tenerife South Airport ☏922 75 93 19, Tenerife North Airport ☏922 25 19 17, Playa de las Américas ☏922 79 23 20,

Puerto de la Cruz ☏922 38 47 19, **Torviscas** ☏922 79 75 65, San Sebastián ☏922 87 04 61; ☏www.hertz.com.

OrCar Tenerife South Airport ☏922 39 22 16, ☏922 39 22 55, Las Américas ☏922 71 42 80, 922 75 37 71 and 922 71 20 68.

La Rueda San Sebastián ☏922 87 07 09, La Playa, Valle Gran Rey ☏922 80 51 97; ☏www.autolarueda.com.

Cycling

Tenerife and La Gomera are mountainous islands and many of the narrow roads are very busy, making neither ideal for leisurely **cycling**. They are, however, well suited to more exciting and satisfying day rides – particularly on dirt roads by **mountain bike**. With the exception of areas within the national park, all hiking trails on **Tenerife** are open to mountain bikes – though many, particularly in the Anaga, are too steep and uneven. The roads of **La Gomera** may be quieter but usually involve extremely tough climbs over the 800-metre passes that separate most major towns. Mountain bikers will, however, be pleased to find that once they've climbed to the high ground of the national park at the centre of the island its trails are open to bikers.

Most carriers **flying** to Tenerife from the UK take bicycles, providing they are packed in a box or bag – available from most bike shops. Bagged bikes are also allowed in the hold of **buses** on both islands, meaning you have the option of cutting out particularly busy parts of a route.

For a private **shuttle service** contact Diga Sports on Tenerife (see p.170) or Bike Station on La Gomera (see p.170), both of whom transport bikes to pretty much anywhere on either island, leaving riders to make their own way back. They also offer **tours** and **bike rental**, as do Fun Factory El Cabezo in El Médano (see p.170) and Mountain Bike Active in Puerto de la Cruz (see p.170). Renting a quality front-suspension mountain bike will set you back around €13 per day, €60 per week.

Bike rental

Las Américas Cycling Diga Sports, Park Club Europe ☎922 79 30 09.

Los Cristianos Bicisport Edificio el Arenal ☎922 75 18 29.

El Médano Fun Factory El Cabezo ☎922 17 62 73.

Puerto de la Cruz Mountain Bike Active, C/Mazaroco, Edif. Daniela 26 ☎922 37 60 81, ⊛Mtb-active.com.

Valle Gran Rey Bike Station, La Puntilla ☎922 80 50 82. Alofi Rentals, La Playa ☎922 80 54 02.

Tours

The many **bus tours** of Tenerife include circular excursions around the island as well as itineraries that typically go to the mountain village of Masca and the Parque Nacional del Teide or Santa Cruz. Prices are generally €20–30. If you're short on time, there are bus trips around La Gomera too (€50), offered from Tenerife's southern resorts. Note that bus trips that seem extraordinarily cheap are most likely to be outings to the restaurants and gift shops that subsidize them and are best avoided.

A deluxe alternative is the thirty-minute flight from Tenerife South Airport with the Canarian Island Helicopter Service (☎922 75 91 51, ⊛www.canarian-helicopter .com). Flights take in the west coast and the cliffs of Los Gigantes before rising up through the Teno for unique views over the national park. At €148 per person, it's pricey but certainly memorable.

Sports and leisure

Tenerife and La Gomera offer a great range of sea- and land-based **activities**, most of which are possible year-round thanks to the archipelago's consistently fine weather. In addition to the natural attractions provided by the waves, winds and mountains, there's been a boom in the popularity of golf on Tenerife.

Surfing and bodyboarding

Though the heavy seas around the islands attract thrill-seeking local **surfers** and **bodyboarders**, only along the accessible Playa de Troya in Las Américas are foreigners happily tolerated. Near to the beach in CC Américas, the K-16 Surf shop (☎922 79 84 84, ⊛k-16surfshop @terra.es) offers gear rental and instruction to absolute beginners and more advanced surfers, from €19 per day.

Windsurfing and kitesurfing

The coast around El Médano (see p.124) is internationally renowned as premium wind- and kitesurfing territory, with inter-national competitions regularly held here. The conditions are often too difficult for beginners, though the Kitecenter Playa Sur (☎922 17 66 88, ⊛www.kitecenter .info) offers instruction for €45 for two hours. You can rent equipment here too or at a number of places around town, including the Fun Factory El Cabezo, in the *Hotel Atlantic Playa* (☎922 17 62 73, ⊛funfactory@teleline.es).

Snorkelling and scuba diving

Some of the more sheltered shores of both islands are suitable for **snorkelling** and there's **scuba diving** at a number of good sites. The underwater scenery and wildlife aren't world-class, but there are plenty of fish – including sharks – and even turtles, and competition between dive schools has made it relatively inexpensive (around €240) to do the basic PADI or CMAS dive courses. The best sites include the spectacular underwater cliffs just south of Los Cristianos, the so-called Stingray City near Las Galletas and a DC3 plane wreck near Puerto de la Cruz.

Scuba diving centres

Costa Adeje Barakuda Club ☎922 74 18 81, ⊛www.divers-net.de/teneriffa.

Garachico Argonaut, C/Esteban Ponte 8 ☎922 83 02 45, ✉argonaut @arrakis.es.

Las Américas Gruber Diving Club, Park Club Europe ☎922 75 27 08, ⊛www.dive-teneriffa.com.

Las Galletas Atlantic Divers, Consuelo Alfonso, Villa Isabel, El Fraile ☎922 73 55 09, ⊛www.atlantic-divers.com; Buceo Tenerif, C/Maria del Carmen Garcia 22 ☎922 73 10 15, ⊛www.buceotenerife.com.

Los Gigantes Los Gigantes Diving Center, Galería de la Marina ☎922 86 04 31, ⊛www.divingtenerife.co.uk.

Puerto de la Cruz Atlantick Diving Centre, Hotel Maritim ☎922 36 28 01.

Valle Gran Rey Fisch & Co, opposite La Playa tourist office ☎922 80 56 88, ⊛www.fischco.de.

Boat trips, deep-sea fishing and sailing

There's a massive array of **boat trips** on offer from Las Américas, Los Cristianos and Los Gigantes, costing from €12. Most head for the Gomeran channel in search of whales and dolphins, while others stop to allow passengers to swim or snorkel along the coast. Some trips are specifically **fishing trips** (from €48 per person for five hours), with deep-sea fishing especially popular. To join the locals fishing off the seashore (which doesn't require a permit), there are plenty of bait and tackle shops – the north coast of the Teno range is one of the best places to test your skills. Chartering a boat is another option and splitting the cost between a group makes the rates more reasonable. WSC, based in Puerto Colón, Las Américas (☎922 71 40 34, ⊛www.tenerife.com/wsc), charges around €400 for three hours on a yacht carrying up to eleven people; eleven-person powerboats are also available for charter (3hr, €550).

Hiking

Puerto de la Cruz is traditionally the resort of choice for hikers on Tenerife. It's well connected by buses and served by a good range of accommodation (and operators offering guided hiking trips), as well as being on the north side of the island where much of the best hiking is to be found. Santa Cruz can also make a good base, as can Los Cristianos if you want to mix hiking with the nightlife, beaches and sunshine of the southern resorts.

Maps and hiking guides are available at bookshops in the island's main towns and resorts, but to save time it's worth picking up information before you head out to Tenerife. Two UK publishers produce useful hiking companions: Sunflower Guides publish two books on Tenerife and one on La Gomera, and Discovery Walking Guides publish folded pamphlets with clear, annotated island maps, as well as books that reprint portions of their map with the addition of further route-finding information.

Hiking companies

Las Américas Diga Sports, Park Club Europe ☎922 79 30 09.

Las Américas, **Los Gigantes** and **Puerto de la Cruz** Sun Holidays ☎609 16 68 50.

Puerto de la Cruz Call Gregorio ☎922 57 28 67; KWA Guided Walks ☎922 37 15 84, ⊛ www.kwa-guiding-tenerife.com.

Valle Gran Rey Timah, La Puntilla ☎922 80 70 37, ⊛www.timah.net.

Climbing

Climbers visiting Tenerife will find over a hundred climbing routes on a rough rock-climbing medium – with lots of pinch grips, pockets and incut edges. Some of the best climbs are in Las Cañadas – in the Parque Nacional del Teide – particularly around Los Roques and La Catedrál.

The recently revised **climbing guide** *Rock Climbs in Majorca, Ibiza and Tenerife* by Chris Craggs should be an essential part of your luggage – it's not available in Tenerife so pick it up before you set off from travel bookshops or online.

Golf

Tenerife's pleasant climate attracts **golf** enthusiasts year-round to its six courses, five of which are dotted around the resorts of southern Tenerife. High season, during the winter months, sees green fees typically hover around €70, while discounts of up to a third are common in the summer. Most courses rent clubs (around €25) and buggies (around €35).

Golf courses

Costa Adeje Golf Costa Adeje ☎922 71 00 00, ⊛www.golfcostaadeje.com, daily 7.30am–7pm.

La Laguna Real Club El Peñón, Guamasa, 2km north of Los Rodeos Airport ☎922 63 66 07, ⊛www.realgolfdetenerife.com, Mon–Fri 8am–12.30pm.

Las Américas Golf Las Américas, autopista Sur Exit 28 ☎922 552 005, ⊛www.golf-tenerife.com, daily 7.40am–7pm.

South Coast Amarilla Golf & Country Golf, San Miguel de Abona, Autopista del Sur Exit 24 ☎922 73 0319, ⊛www.amarillagolf .es, daily 7.30am–7.30pm; Golf del Sur, San Miguel de Abona; Autopista del Sur Exit 24 ☎922 73 81 70, ⊛www .golfdelsur.net. Daily 10.30am–7pm; Palos, Carretera Guaza, Las Galletas, km. 7 Exit 26 from Autopista Sur ☎922 73 00 80, wwww.golflospalos.com, daily 8am–8pm.

Spectator sports

Traditional Canarian sports such as wrestling and stick fighting are undergoing a renaissance on Tenerife, but it's **football** that attracts most local atten-

tion. Times are hard for Club Deportivo Tenerife as they languish in the second division, so to offer support, head for the Estadio Heliodoro Rodríguez López (ticket office Mon–Fri 10am–1pm & 5–8pm; ☎922 29 16 99 or 922 24 06 13), where seats cost €36, standing €11 and are usually available on match days.

Any sizeable place is likely to have a ring for contests of **Canarian wrestling** (*Lucha Canaria*) and information on fixtures can be gained from the Federación de Lucha Canaria, Callejón del Capitán Brotons 7, Santa Cruz (☎922 25 14 52), where bouts are held on Friday and Saturday evenings. This relatively non-violent sport involves two barefoot men in a round, sandy ring attempting, by gripping the bottom of the opponent's shorts, to manoeuvre each other to the ground. Kicks and punches are not allowed. There are three rounds and winning two secures a point for the victor's twelve-man team. Bouts continue until one team has the twelve points it needs to win, and the whole contest can take around three hours.

A more minor tradition, and one primarily making appearances as a demonstration sport at fiestas, is **stick fighting** (*juego del palo*). This contest, a derivative of Guanche stick-and-stone duels, uses large, two-metre-long staffs to both attack and defend, with the aim of trying to knock an opponent off his perch on a relatively small flat rock.

Festivals and events

January 1
New Year's Day A Spanish public holiday, New Year's Day is traditionally greeted with fireworks and the eating of a grape at every chime.

January 6
Reyes Magos (Three Kings). A public holiday, celebrated with processions in major towns the day before. This, rather than December 25, is traditionally the day for present giving.

January 20
Fiesta de San Sebastián (La Gomera) Singing and dancing to celebrate the town's patron saint.

February/March
Carnival The biggest event of the year. Festivities begin in Santa Cruz (see box), before moving on to other large towns, most notably Puerto de la Cruz.

Late March/early April
Easter week (Semana Santa) Jueves Santo (Maundy Thursday) and Viernes Santo (Good Friday) are both public holidays in Spain and elaborate processions take place on both days in La Laguna, a one a silent procession of religious brotherhoods.

Santa Cruz's Carnival

Santa Cruz's **Carnival** is one of Europe's most vibrant and colourful festivals, attracting up to 280,000 people.

Though originally following the religious calendar, the event has now extended deep into Lent itself and each night the Plaza de España and surrounding streets fill with revellers dancing until dawn. Costumes are almost compulsory and many dress in the annual theme.

The highlight of the week is the **Grand Procession** on Shrove Tuesday – a cavalcade of floats, bands, dancers and entertainers, who march and dance their way along the dockside road. Also popular is the **Burial of the Sardine** on Ash Wednesday, when the effigy of a sardine is burnt before wailing widows. Traditionally, the sardine's cremation signified the last day of the carnival but the finale actually comes the following weekend – at which point smaller towns around the island often start their own celebrations.

For the latest on the current year's preparations and plans check ⓦwww .carnavaltenerife.com.

April 25
Fiesta de San Marcos, Agulo (La Gomera) A statue of Agulo's patron saint, San Marcos, is surrounded by bonfires through which local young men run in a test of courage.

May
Romeriás Harvest festivals taking place throughout the month in the Orotava Valley.

May 3
Dia de Santa Cruz Festival celebrating the founding of Tenerife's capital with a procession and lots of traditional entertainment, including Canarian wrestling.

May 30
Canary Islands' Day Public holiday marked by folk dances In the plazas of Santa Cruz.

May/June
Corpus Christi On the Thursday that follows the eighth Sunday after Easter, Corpus Christi is celebrated all over Tenerife. Major events are held in La Laguna and, a week later, in La Orotava – where streets are covered in floral carpets.

June 13–29
Los Piques Celebrated in Agulo, La Gomera, this festival includes quarrels in the whistling language, El Silbo.

June 23 & 24
Fiesta de San Juan Herds of goats from the surrounding area are bathed in the harbour at Puerto de la Cruz as part of the midsummer celebrations.

First Sunday of July
Romería de San Benito Abad Celebrations in La Laguna including a major religious procession.

July 16
Fiesta Virgen del Carmen The largest celebrations for the patron saint of fishermen and sailors are in Santa Cruz and Puerto de la Cruz on Tenerife, and in Valle Gran Rey and Playa de Santiago on La Gomera. Celebrations usually include a procession of boats.

July 25
Santiago Day Public holiday in honour of St James the Apostle, patron saint of Spain. The Virgin of Candelaria (see p.71) is paraded in fine robes adorned with gold and surrounded by folk dances and offerings of flowers. Major festivities take place in Santa Cruz too, with citizens also celebrating the anniversary of the defeat of Nelson and his British fleet.

August
Romería de San Roque in Garachico Dates vary for this, one of the largest and most spectacular harvest and folk festivals on Tenerife.

August 15
Fiesta Virgen de la Candelaria The patron saint of the archipelago shares her

day with *Beñasmen*, a Guanche harvest festival – which explains the flowers, greenery, sheep and goats that are paraded behind the statue of the virgin.

September 6
Fiesta de Cristobal Colón Anniversary of the departure of Columbus (Colón) from San Sebastián, La Gomera, on his first voyage to the Americas.

September 7
Fiesta de la Virgen del Socorro Güimar puts on a large procession from the church to the sea in honour of the town's patron saint.

September 7–15
Fiesta del Santísimo Cristo Lengthy religious festival in La Laguna that includes

a procession behind a fifteenth-century Gothic carving of Christ on the Cross, given to the island's conqueror, Alonso de Lugo.

November 1
All Saints Day Public holiday with fiestas in towns around Tenerife.

November 29
Fiesta del Vino Wine festival in Icod and Puerto de la Cruz to celebrate the grape harvest. The highlight is kamikaze sledding (sleds were once used to transport the harvest), with Icod's course the steepest and most dangerous.

December 25
Navidad Christmas Day is a public holiday.

Directory

Accommodation Though accommodation on Tenerife is plentiful, much of it consists of hotel and apartment complexes given over to package tours. Of these, we have listed those that accept independent bookings, though in many cases walk-in rates are substantially higher than pre-booked package prices. There's also a small stock of family-run pensions and smaller hotels in the main towns and resorts, and a couple of campsites.

The situation in La Gomera is geared more to independent travel and small, inexpensive apartment blocks have emerged to meet demand. Throughout the Places chapters, prices listed are for the cheapest double room in high season, but excluding Christmas and New Year when rates rocket. In the case of apartments that sleep more than two, the price for the smallest available unit per night is given. Travellers wanting to stay a week or more are likely to find the nightly rate can be reduced a little. Both islands also have a good stock of *casas rurales*: attractive old renovated houses in the countryside that are rented out as self-catering holiday accommodation. Typically a week in one of these will cost from £200 for a one- to two-bedroom place. The Internet is ideal for finding this kind of accommodation – try Acantur @www.ecoturismocanarias

.com/Canarias/uk/islas.htm; Aecan @www.aecan.com; and Top Rural @www.toprural.net.

Addresses Common abbreviations are: C/ for Calle (street); Ctra for Carretera (main road); Avda for Avenida (avenue); Edif for Edificio (a large block), and CC for Centro Commercial (a shopping centre or mall, often in an Edificio). An address given as C/Flores 24, 3° means third floor, 24 Flores Street. Derecha and izquierda mean right- and left-hand apartment or office.

Airlines Britannia ☎922 75 91 34, @www.britanniaairways.com; British Airways ☎914 36 59 00, @www.ba.com; Iberia ☎922 75 92 85, @www.iberia.com; Monarch ☎922 75 93 98, @www.fly-crown.com.

Banks and exchange The currency in the Canary Islands is the euro (€). Bank branches, many with ATMs, are plentiful in all the main towns and resorts. Opening hours are Mon–Fri 9am–2pm, Sat 9am–1pm – except between late May and September when banks close on Saturday, and during the Carnival period (February or March) when they close at midday. Outside these times, it's usually possible to change cash at larger hotels, exchange booths and, in resort areas, with real-estate or travel agents. Hotel rates are usually poor, but exchange booths and agents sometimes give better rates than the banks.

Complaints All hotels, restaurants and other businesses have a complaints book (*hoja de reclamación*) in which complaints can be logged. Noted in this form, complaints are treated extremely seriously by authorities and therefore should be used as a last resort.

Consulates Britain, Plaza de Weyler, Santa Cruz de Tenerife ☎922 28 68 63; Ireland, C/Castillo 8, 4ºA, Santa Cruz de Tenerife ☎922 24 56 71. The nearest US consulate is on the neighbouring island of Gran Canaria at Los Martínez de Escober 3, Oficina 7, Las Palmas de Gran Canaria ☎928 27 12 59. The nearest representation for most other countries is in Madrid.

Customs The current limits on what can be brought back to the UK are 2 litres of non-sparkling wine, 1 litre of spirits, 60ml of perfume, 50ml cologne, 200 cigarettes and up to £145 of other goods and gifts.

Emergency services For police, ambulance and fire brigade call ☎112.

Hospitals Hospital de Nuestra Señora de la Candelaria, on the TF-5 motorway between Santa Cruz and La Laguna ☎922 27 55 63; Clinica Tamaragua, Agustin de Béthencourt 30, Puerto de la Cruz ☎922 38 05 12; Hospital Las Américas, Southern Las Américas ☎922 78 07 59; Hospital El Calvario, San Sebastián ☎922 87 04 50.

Internet Every major town and resort on both Tenerife and La Gomera has at least one café with Internet connections where half an hour on line usually costs around €2.

Karting The Karting Club de Tenerife (☎922 730 703) has a free shuttle bus from Las Américas to get you – and the kids – to its international standard track.

Mail The postal system in the Canary Islands is quite slow and it usually takes at least ten days for a postcard or letter to reach the UK or mainland Europe (outside Spain). As well as the post offices, most shops selling postcards sell **stamps** (*sellos*). **Post offices** can be found in all the main towns and villages and are open Mon–Fri 8.30am–2.30pm & Sat 9.30am–1pm.

Pharmacies *Farmacias* are indicated by a large green cross and open Mon–Fri 9am–1pm & 4–8pm, Sat 9am–1pm). Additionally, pharmacies in each area have a rota to provide 24-hour emergency cover, details of which are posted on any pharmacy door.

Telephones Most hotels add surcharges to calls made from rooms, so it's cheaper to use one of the many coin- or card-operated **payphones**. Various companies offer **phone cards** – available from newsagents, petrol stations and convenience stores – and while some work out cheaper than feeding in euros, it's worth checking the small print to see if there's a connection fee. **Mobile phones** work in the Canary Islands but check with your service provider about coverage and call costs.

Time Both islands are in the same time zone as the UK and Ireland, making them five hours ahead of the US East Coast and eleven hours behind East Coast Australia.

Tipping In bars and taxis, rounding up to the next euro is fine, while with waiters and hairdressers a 5–10 per cent tip is perfectly adequate.

Language

Spanish

Once you get into it, **Spanish** is the easiest language there is, and you'll be helped everywhere by people who are eager to try and understand even the most faltering attempt. English is spoken in the main tourist areas, but you'll get a far better reception if you try communicating with Canarian Islanders in their own tongue.

For more than a brief introduction to the language, pick up a copy of the Rough Guide **Spanish Dictionary Phrasebook**.

Pronunciation

The rules of **pronunciation** are pretty straightforward and strictly observed.

A   somewhere between the A sound of back and that of father.
E   as in get.
I   as in police.
O   as in hot.
U   as in rule.
C   is spoken like an S before E and I, hard otherwise: *cerca* is pronounced "sairka" (standard Spanish would pronounce it "thairka").
G   is a guttural H sound (like the ch in loch) before E or I, a hard G elsewhere – *gigante* becomes "higante".
H   is always silent.
J   is the same as a guttural G: *jamón* is "hamon".
LL sounds like an English Y: *tortilla* is pronounced "torteeya".
N   is as in English unless it has a tilde (accent) over it, when it becomes NY: *mañana* sounds like "manyana".
QU is pronounced like an English K.
R   is rolled, RR doubly so.
V   sounds more like B, *vino* becoming "beano".
X   has an S sound before consonants, normal X before vowels.
Z   is the same as a soft C, so *cerveza* becomes "thairbaitha".

Words and phrases

Basics			
Yes, No, OK	Sí, No, Vale	Now, Later	Ahora, Más tarde
Please, Thank you	Por favor, Gracias	Open, Closed	Abierto/a, Cerrado/a
Where?, When?	¿Dónde?, ¿Cuando?	With, Without	Con, Sin
What?, How much?	¿Qué?, ¿Cuánto?	Good, Bad	Buen(o)/a, Mal(o)/a
Here, There	Aquí, Allí	Big, Small	Gran(de), Pequeño/a
This, That	Esto, Eso	Cheap, Expensive	Barato, Caro
		Hot, Cold	Caliente, Frío
		More, Less	Más, Menos

Today, Tomorrow	Hoy, Mañana
Yesterday	Ayer
The bill	La cuenta

Greetings and responses

Hello, Goodbye	Hola, Adiós
Good morning	Buenos días
Good afternoon/ night	Buenas tardes/ noches
See you later	Hasta luego
Sorry	Lo siento/disculpe
Excuse me	Con permiso/perdón
How are you?	¿Como está (usted)?
I (don't) understand	(No) Entiendo
Not at all/ You're welcome	De nada
Do you speak English?	¿Habla (usted) inglés?
I (don't) speak Spanish	(No) Hablo español
My name is . . .	Me llamo. . .
What's your name?	¿Como se llama usted?
I am English / Scottish / Welsh / Australian / Canadian / American / Irish / New Zealander	Soy inglés(a) / escocés(a) / galés(a) / australiano(a) / canadiense(a) / americano(a) / irlandés(a) / Nueva Zelandes(a)

Hotels, transport and directions

I want	Quiero
I'd like	Quisiera
Do you know. . .?	¿Sabe . . .?
I don't know	No sé
There is (is there)?	(¿)Hay(?)
Give me (one like that)	Deme (uno así)
Do you have. . .?	¿Tiene . . .?
. . . the time	. . . la hora
. . . a room	. . . una habitación
. . . with two beds/ double bed	. . . con dos camas /cama matrimonial
. . . with shower/ bath	. . . con ducha/baño
It's for one person	Es para una persona
For one night	para una noche
For one week	para una semana
How do I get to. . .?	¿Por donde se va a . . .?

Left, right, straight on	Izquierda, derecha, todo recto
Where is. . .?	¿Dónde está . . .?
. . . the bus station	. . . la estación de guaguas
. . . the nearest bank	. . . el banco mas cercano
. . . the post office	. . . el correos/la oficina de correos
. . . the toilet	. . . el baño
Where does the bus to . . . leave from?	De dónde sale la guagua para. . .?
I'd like a (return) ticket to . . .	Quisiera un billete (de ida y vuelta) para. . .
What time does it leave?	¿A qué hora sale?

Numbers and days

1	un/uno/una
2	dos
3	tres
4	cuatro
5	cinco
6	seis
7	siete
8	ocho
9	nueve
10	diez
11	once
12	doce
13	trece
14	catorce
15	quince
16	diez y seis
17	diez y siete
20	veinte
21	veintiuno
30	treinta
40	cuarenta
50	cincuenta
60	sesenta
70	setenta
80	ochenta
90	noventa
100	cien(to)
101	ciento uno
200	doscientos
500	quinientos
1000	mil
Monday	lunes
Tuesday	martes
Wednesday	miércoles

Thursday	jueves
Friday	viernes
Saturday	sábado
Sunday	domingo
today	hoy
yesterday	ayer
tomorrow	mañana

Food and drink

aceitunas	olives
agua	water
ahumados	smoked fish
al ajillo	with olive oil and garlic
a la marinera	seafood cooked with garlic, onions and white wine
a la parilla	charcoal-grilled
a la plancha	grilled on a hot plate
a la romana	fried in batter
albóndigas	meatballs
almejas	clams
anchoas	anchovies
arroz	rice
asado	roast
bacalao	cod
berenjena	aubergine/eggplant
bocadillo	bread roll sandwich
boquerones	small, anchovy-like fish, usually served in vinegar
café (con leche)	(white) coffee
calamares	squid
cangrejo	crab
cebolla	onion
cerveza	beer
champiñones	mushrooms
chorizo	spicy sausage
croquetas	croquettes, usually with bits of ham in
cuchara	spoon
cuchillo	knife
empanada	slices of fish/meat pie
ensalada	salad
ensaladilla	russian salad (diced vegetables in mayonnaise, often with tuna)
fresa	strawberry
gambas	prawns

gofio	finely ground mix of wheat, barley or maize, usually accompanying soups and stews
hígado	liver
huevos	eggs
jamón serrano	cured ham
jamón de york	regular ham
langostinos	langoustines
lechuga	lettuce
manzana	apple
mejillones	mussels
mojo	garlic dressing available in "rojo" (spicy "red" version) and "verde" ("green", made with coriander)
naranja	orange
ostras	oysters
pan	bread
papas arrugadas	unpeeled new potatoes, boiled dry in salted water
papas alioli	potatoes in garlic mayonnaise
papas bravas	fried potatoes in a spicy tomato sauce
pimientos	peppers
pimientos de padrón	small peppers, with the odd hot one
piña	pineapple
pisto	assortment of cooked vegetables, similar to ratatouille
plátano	banana
pollo	chicken
pulpo	octopus
queso	cheese
salchicha	sausage
setas	oyster mushrooms
sopa	soup
té	tea
tenedor	fork
tomate	tomato
tortilla española	potato omelette
tortilla francesa	plain omelette
vino (blanco/ rosado/tinto)	(white/rosé/red) wine
zarzuela	Canarian fish stew
zumo	juice

Glossary

avenida	avenue
barranco	gorge
barrio	suburb or neighbourhood
calle	(usually abbreviated to C/) street or road
CC (centro comercial)	shopping and entertainment mall
edificio	building
ermita	hermitage
hacienda	large manor house
guagua	local name for buses
Guanche	original inhabitants of the Canary Islands
iglesia	church
menú del día	daily menu in a restaurant
mercado	market
mirador	view point
Mudéjar	Spanish-Moorish architecture
parador	state-run hotel, usually housed in buildings of historic interest
playa	beach
plaza	square
terraza	temporary summer outdoor bar/club

ROUGH GUIDES
TRAVEL SERIES

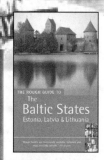

THE ROUGH GUIDE TO
The Baltic States
Estonia, Latvia & Lithuania

THE ROUGH GUIDE TO
China

THE ROUGH GUIDE TO
Florida

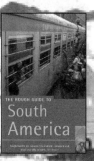

THE ROUGH GUIDE TO
South America

THE ROUGH GUIDE TO
Sweden

THE ROUGH GUIDE TO
USA

THE ROUGH GUIDE TO
Vietnam

THE ROUGH GUIDE TO
Vancouver
With Victoria, Whistler and the Sunshine Coast

THE ROUGH GUIDE TO
The Philippines

Travel guides to more than
250 destinations
from Alaska to Zimbabwe
smooth travel

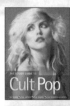

Index and small print

A Rough Guide to Rough Guides

Tenerife DIRECTIONS is published by Rough Guides. The first *Rough Guide to Greece*, published in 1982, was a student scheme that became a publishing phenomenon. The immediate success of the book – with numerous reprints and a Thomas Cook prize shortlisting – spawned a series that rapidly covered dozens of destinations. Rough Guides had a ready market among low budget backpackers, but soon also acquired a much broader and older readership that relished Rough Guides' wit and inquisitiveness as much as their enthusiastic, critical approach. Everyone wants value for money, but not at any price. Rough Guides soon began supplementing the "rougher" information about hostels and low-budget listings with the kind of detail on restaurants and quality hotels that independent-minded visitors on any budget might expect, whether on business in New York or trekking in Thailand. These days the guides offer recommendations from shoestring to luxury and a large number of destinations around the globe, including almost every country in the Americas and Europe, more than half of Africa and most of Asia and Australasia. Rough Guides now publish:

- Travel guides to more than 200 worldwide destinations
- Dictionary phrasebooks to 22 major languages
- Maps printed on rip-proof and waterproof Polyart™ paper
- Music guides running the gamut from Opera to Elvis
- Reference books on topics as diverse as the Weather and Shakespeare
- World Music CDs in association with World Music Network

Visit **www.roughguides.com** to see our latest publications.

Publishing Information

This 1st edition published August 2004 by
Rough Guides Ltd, 80 Strand, London WC2R 0RL.
345 Hudson St, 4th Floor, New York, NY 10014,
USA.

Distributed by the Penguin Group
Penguin Books Ltd, 80 Strand, London WC2R 0RL
Penguin Group (USA), 375 Hudson Street, NY
10014, USA
Penguin Group (Australia), 487 Maroondah
Highway, PO Box 257, Ringwood, Victoria 3134,
Australia
Penguin Group (Canada), 10 Alcorn Avenue,
Toronto, Ontario, Canada M4V 1E4
Penguin Group (NZ), 182–190 Wairau Road,
Auckland 10, New Zealand
Typeset in Bembo and Helvetica to an original
design by Henry Iles.
Printed and bound in Italy by Graphicom

192pp includes index
A catalogue record for this book is available from
the British Library

ISBN 1-84353-323-5

The publishers and authors have done their best to
ensure the accuracy and currency of all the information
in **Tenerife DIRECTIONS**, however, they
can accept no responsibility for any loss, injury, or
inconvenience sustained by any traveller as a result
of information or advice contained in the guide.

1   3   5   7   9   8   6   4   2

Help us update

We've gone to a lot of effort to ensure that the first edition of **Tenerife DIRECTIONS** is accurate and up-to-date. However, things change – places get "discovered", opening hours are notoriously fickle, restaurants and rooms raise prices or lower standards. If you feel we've got it wrong or left something out, we'd like to know, and if you can remember the address, the price, the time, the phone number, so much the better.

We'll credit all contributions, and send a copy of the next edition (or any other DIRECTIONS guide or Rough Guide if you prefer) for the best letters. Everyone who writes to us and isn't already a subscriber will receive a copy of our full-colour thrice-yearly newsletter. Please mark letters: **"Tenerife DIRECTIONS Update"** and send to: Rough Guides, 80 Strand, London WC2R 0RL, or Rough Guides, 4th Floor, 345 Hudson St, New York, NY 10014. Or send an email to **mail@roughguides.com**

Have your questions answered and tell others about your trip at **www.roughguides.atinfopop.com**

Rough Guide Credits

Text editor: Clifton Wilkinson
Layout: Andy Hilliard
Photography: Christian Williams
Cartography: Map Studio, Katie Lloyd-Jones, Miles Irving

Picture editor: Joe Mee, Mark Thomas
Proofreader: Ken Bell
Production: Julia Bovis
Design: Henry Iles
Cover art direction: Louise Boulton

SMALL PRINT

The author

Despite falling into the Atlantic off the coast of Tenerife as a toddler, in 1998 Christian Williams returned to the island, undeterred, to research and write his first travel guide. He's been working with Rough Guides ever since and has co-authored their guides to Skiing and Snowboarding in North America, the US Rocky Mountains and Canada.

Acknowledgements

The author wishes to thank those people on Tenerife who helped to make the book as accurate as possible and for all the others for knowing how to throw a good party. Praise is especially due to the ever-helpful Silvana, queen of the seas; the multilingual salsa king Julio César; Chix and Rachel for bringing B52s to La Gomera; and Judy for her appreciation of great spaces. At Rough Guides thanks go to Helena Smith, Kate Berens, Geoff Howard, Sharon Martins and Joe Mee, but particularly to Clifton Wilkinson for his sterling efforts at the editorial desk, where he worked with admirable attention to detail, pulling things together in largely uncharted waters.

Index

Map entries are marked in **colour**

INDEX

INDEX